The Secular Priesthood in England and Wales: History, Mission and Identity

Judith Champ

Oscott Publications

First published in 2016 by Oscott Publications

© St Mary's College, Oscott and Judith Champ

Oscott College
Chester Road
Sutton Coldfield
West Midlands
B73 5AA

Tel. 0121 321 5000
www.oscott.net

ISBN 978-0-9933991-1-4

Cover design: Rev. Simon J. Baker

Text design and layout: Pixel Press

Printed by Genprint (Ireland) Ltd

Publishing Consultant and Index: Fergus Mulligan, www.publishing.ie

Contents

Foreword

This book blends, in an unusual way, the study of the history of English Catholic life since the Reformation, and insight into the life and ministry of the secular priesthood today. It appears at a particularly apt moment, as we move towards the celebration of the four hundred and fiftieth anniversary of the founding of the English College, Douai. That foundation, in 1568, launched the beginning of the mission of the secular priesthood in England after the Reformation, which secured the survival and revival of Catholic life.

This book is both a timely reminder of the history and traditions of priesthood in this country, but also a stimulus to new ways of thinking, based on new conversations, which will take us into the future. It reminds us of the importance of the missionary identity of the secular priesthood in England and Wales, not only in the past, but in our own time, and in the coming generation.

It illustrates the flexibility, and the capacity to embrace change, that secured the revival of Catholic life, to which we all owe so much. We too will need to be flexible and to be open to change in order to take the Church forward and respond to constant challenges. We owe it to the priests who have gone before us to live up to their legacy. This book emphasises something that we all need to remember in the Church, quoting Pope Francis, that 'service and mission flow from a sense of history', from 'being men and women of history, by understanding that the story does not begin or end with me'.

I warmly commend this book. It is an important resource for us today. In particular I encourage every priest to read it and reflect on the vision and challenges it presents. An understanding of our great heritage can help us to shape our future!

+ Vincent
Cardinal Vincent Nichols
Archbishop of Westminster

Preface

This book has emerged from many years of research and writing on the history of English Catholicism, in the context of seminary teaching and formation. Working in a seminary that plays an intrinsic part in the history and tradition of the Church in England and Wales has enabled me to understand at first hand the ways in which history informs the present. It is a unique experience, and a great blessing, to be involved in the formation of priests in an institution founded for this purpose over two hundred years ago. It is impossible not to be conscious of the historical identity of the secular priesthood, when it is a part of everyday life.

Colleagues and seminarians, past and present, have all played a part in the gestation of this book, and in a real sense, it is their book. It is about their history and their future, and I venture to dedicate it to them.

It is an invitation to celebrate the great tradition of pastoral ministry into which the present generation steps. In 2018, there will be an opportunity to rejoice, and to thank God for the priests who have led the Church in England and Wales since the foundation of the English College, Douai. This book sketches some aspects of the history of the continuity and transformation of the identity of the Catholic priesthood in England and Wales since then.

It is, however, as much about the future of the priesthood as about the past.

Judith Champ
June 2016

Introduction:
An Identity Rooted
in History

But those who wait for the Lord will renew their strength.
They will soar on wings like eagles; they will run and not
be weary; they will walk and not grow faint.

(Isaiah 40: 31)

The inspiration for this book is rooted in history, but it is primarily about what lies ahead. It embodies both a recognition and a celebration of the past, and a proclamation of hope for the future. Identity is inextricably connected to history; that is where our roots lie, whether in our family, or in the shared experience of an ethnic or religious group, of a nation, or a city, town or village. We share a communal identity, which incorporates roles, functions, skills and routines, and embraces shared beliefs, attitudes, values, and historical origin, as well as being possessed of a personal identity, which distinguishes us as individuals within the larger culture.[1] Dislocation from history is disorientating, leading to fragmentation and an impoverished sense of both communal and personal identity.

Catholicism has ancient historical roots in England and Wales, but many of them were torn up in the sixteenth century, leaving new traditions and a new culture to grow within the Established Church. The building of a minority Catholic community after the Reformation was by no means an obvious option, and difficult choices had to be made. Priestly identity, as described in *Pastores Dabo Vobis*,[2] the Church's most recent teaching document on priesthood, is shaped by the spiritual and pastoral choices made over the course of the history of the local Church, and how those choices have been understood and interpreted.[3]

The choices made in the last five hundred years or so shaped a new set of traditions and a new identity for Catholicism in English society, and particularly for the priesthood, and they need to be understood and reinterpreted afresh. The secular, or diocesan, priesthood of England and Wales has a rich and distinctive identity, which draws upon the unique history of the Church in this country. Understanding of the relationship between the identity of the secular priesthood, and the history that shaped it, has become weakened, or even lost in recent years. This loss is damaging, not only the priesthood of the present day, but the life of our parishes, and the discernment of vocations to the priesthood.

It is almost four hundred and fifty years since the foundation of the English College in Douai, in 1568, which trained the first generations of secular priests for the mission in England and Wales after the Reformation. The founding of Douai marked the necessary new beginning for the Church, if it was to survive in England and Wales. It began the creation of a new type of priesthood, based on a different understanding of what it meant to be a secular priest. It was not a one-off reinvention, but the first hesitant step on a journey of discovery.

That journey is not only historically significant, but offers a road map for the future. Recent generations have seen some hopeful turnings but also some lost paths and dead ends. The four hundred and fiftieth anniversary of the foundation of Douai, in 2018 is a moment to celebrate the English secular priesthood, and to renew its historic missionary identity.

This moment of celebration, and of renewed attentiveness to a distinctive tradition, offers an opportunity to rediscover the past, and renew the spirit that sustained the Catholic community in times of change, and to stimulate hope for the future. Now is the time for the secular priesthood in England and Wales to be inspired afresh, by reflecting on experience in the light of the powerful tradition of which it is a part. A rediscovered sense of communal identity can help the secular priesthood to renew itself, and, therefore, the whole Catholic community, bishops, priests and lay faithful, with fresh hope and vision. A confident vision for the future, however, needs to be embedded in a renewed understanding of the past.

The Medieval Inheritance

*Day unto day takes up the story and night unto night
makes known the message.*
(Psalm 18: 3)

The term 'secular priest' has a chequered history, although it has been in common usage for hundreds of years. Originally, it was a pejorative term, used by early medieval monks to distinguish themselves as 'regulars' from the parochial clergy who lived in the world rather than in cloistered communities. It gradually lost its negative connotations, and came to denote the priests who lived and worked outside the cloister, in close everyday contact with the people among whom they lived. The secular priest was central to the emergent parochial structures of the Church.

Pope Gregory the Great, revered as the 'Apostle of the English', for sending St Augustine of Canterbury to these shores in the sixth century, laid down basic pastoral norms for clerics. Alfred, King of the West Saxons, translated and circulated them, ensuring that they were familiar in England by the end of the first Christian millennium.

Gregory expected a priest to give a good example by his life, not to seek worldly prosperity, and to be merciful and caring towards his people. He should take care for his own spiritual life as well as that of others, ensuring that he was not too busy for 'the things that are within, lest either he fall away from his inmost concerns, or bestow not on his neighbours what he owes them'. Preaching was important, but the priest should 'give forth a sound more by his deeds than by his words, and rather by good living imprint footsteps for men to follow than by speaking shew them the way to walk in'.[4] Pope Gregory's principles formed the basis of the pastoral responsibilities of the secular clergy, who sustained the Christian life of the great majority of lay people. They continue to this day to underpin the Church's expectations of the secular priest.

By the time of the Norman Conquest, the secular clergy in England were a distinctive group, separate from the monks and living alongside the parish churches and their parishioners.

> Because of their role out in the world ministering to the laity, the secular clergy were arguably more important than any other group in maintaining and deepening the influence of Christianity on society as a whole.[5]

Secular priests were deeply rooted in society, forming the bridge that connected the lay faithful with God. That role, as the bridge to the divine, was reinforced by ways in which the Church began to distinguish between its expectations of a priest and of a lay person.

The Church moved towards insisting that the secular priest, while living in the midst of his parishioners, led a radically different way of life from his neighbours. Freed from worldly concerns, this meant separation from family, kinship ties and other concerns, and the requirement to live a celibate life. While the social, economic and religious distinction between clergy and laity became established, the physical proximity and interaction between the parish priest and the people in his care became very close. This meant that, in pre-Reformation England, the secular clergy occupied a position at the very heart of everyday life, as well as being central to the practice of faith.

The complexity of the relationship between priest and laity was enhanced by the Fourth Lateran Council, which in 1215, effectively defined a new concept of priesthood, insisting that holy orders placed a man in a different human condition from that of the laity. As a consequence, the Church placed greater insistence on clerical education, but for most priests, the priority was the pastoral requirements of parish life. Most of them received a very basic education prior to ordination, which rarely, in practice, matched the expectations imposed by the Fourth Lateran Council.

Poverty of clerical education became a long-running source of complaint in medieval England. Local schools, often run by clergy themselves, provided some basic level of education, but the quality, content and longevity of it varied widely. No-one was marked for priesthood until adulthood, so the early education of priests was the same as that of their neighbours, until preparation for ordination. Only cathedrals and monasteries provided more advanced clerical education, and it was not until the fifteenth century that there was much improvement in what was provided in England.[6]

The Fourth Lateran Council also placed greater emphasis on the sacramental life of the Church, regulating sacramental confession and the Eucharist, and insisting on the participation of the priest in celebrating marriage and baptism. These developments secured the unique role of the priest in the minds of parishioners. The celebration of Mass became his daily privilege and duty, and his authority to celebrate the Eucharist and to handle the sacred elements gave him a quasi-divine power. Yet he continued to live at close quarters with his neighbours, and to become even more intimately involved in their lives.

The Council's institution of the obligation on the laity to make their confession to their parish priest, at least annually, gave the parochial clergy a powerful pastoral and catechetical tool. It offered the opportunity, not only to explore the moral condition of penitents, but also their knowledge of Catholic faith and practice. Confessors were instructed to examine penitents on their familiarity with basic prayers and on the articles of the Creed. The annual requirement of sacramental confession led gradually to greater frequency of confession among the more pious and educated, and increased the expectations that the Church made of the clergy.

Confessional practice and catechesis became closely linked. A growing literature, designed to help the clergy to instruct the laity, both responded to, and prompted, increasing lay demands for spiritual guidance. The relationship became intensified, as priests had to make judgements about when and what should be confessed, what was trivial or serious, and what were appropriate penances or cures for spiritual and moral difficulties. This was all governed by the work of St Raymond Penyafort, who, in the decade after the Fourth Lateran Council, compiled what was, effectively, the first Code of Canon Law. His *Summa de Poenitentiae* of 1234 spawned hundreds of confessional manuals for the use of parish priests.

The significance of the English manuals, written between the thirteenth and fifteenth centuries is reflected in the most famous literary legacy of medieval England, Chaucer's *Canterbury Tales*. Among all the hostile and often scatological references to friars, monks and other religious professionals, the parson is portrayed as an exemplary figure, and a truly virtuous man. The last of Chaucer's pilgrims to speak, the parson refuses to tell a fictional tale, preferring to offer instead a pious homily on sin, confession and repentance, based on a manual. By Chaucer's time, in the 1340s, the content of manuals was obviously familiar in England.

The priest's doctrinal control, his oversight of morality, and judgement of worthiness to receive sacraments revolutionised what it meant to be a secular priest, and demanded qualities that far outstripped those anticipated by Gregory the Great. The relationship between clergy and laity became increasingly complex. Although control of sacramental life placed him at the centre of the Church's disciplinary system, and gave him considerable authority over behaviour and morality, this was counterbalanced by the reality that the laity had the power of the purse.

It was his penitents who endowed the altars, statues, screens and furnishings amidst which a priest ministered, and there was a sense of intimacy and ownership between parishioners and their local church. Wealthier laity exercised rights of patronage, and control over benefices, which could limit the independent control over parish life exercised by parish priests, archdeacons and bishops. The secular clergy only exercised authority as long as the people acknowledged and accepted it.

High standards of clerical life were expected, both by bishops and by the laity, and failures caused conflict. Complaints recorded in visitation reports and court cases centred on greed and avarice, where tithes and burial fees were concerned, on sexual incontinence, although much of that could be malicious gossip, and on general lack of charity, which could simply mean an unwelcome harsh word. Recorded evidence of failings, rather than routine successes, is, inevitably, easier to find.

On the whole, medieval English priests were doing a reasonable job, which was no small achievement, given the inherent tensions and contradictions in a role that placed the priest at the very hub of local society. He not only served families in sacramental situations, but kept note of their kinship, dowries, wills and places of burial, said Masses for the living and the dead, defended people and their possessions from unwarranted interference, and from the devil, witches and curses. He was the teacher, judge, arbitrator, reconciler and solver of disputes, and was responsible for the maintenance of the church and churchyard as a place of public, communal holiness. Disputes between clergy and laity were certainly common, but so was social conflict generally, and few priests had the capacity to distance themselves from the rough and tumble of communal disputes.

An English secular priest living in the first decade of the sixteenth century stood in a long tradition of parish clergy, whose role had emerged over a thousand years. He lived at the centre of the parochial system, and his role within the community was secured by the law of the Church and by popular expectations. The ties between the parish and the priest were strongly governed by social pressures, as much as by canon law, and within this tight social network, a distinctive and separate clerical caste had emerged. Perceptions of what was expected of the priest were enhanced throughout the late medieval period, and Church leaders were increasingly critical of the systemic failure to prevent unsuitable men from being ordained. The late medieval priest was, in short, a product of the society in which he had been born and brought up.

Accusations of clerical lack of piety, poor morality, neglect of duties and worldliness, all suggesting weak preparation for ordination, were rife. 'One of the starting points for many studies of the Reformation in England has been the lamentable state of the English clergy at the time.'[7] This has been somewhat overstated, and recent historians have adjusted the level of criticism, to take account of social realities. Nichols' picture of little vigour or excitement, little strong meat in spiritual formation in parishes, but rather, a thorough and sincere attempt to keep things going, which did little to inspire, is probably closer to the truth. English secular clergy on the eve of the Reformation were neither illiterate nor incompetent, but were, in many cases inadequately educated and ignorant of the new learning that was revolutionising Europe.

The Collapse of the Old Order

Foundations once destroyed, what can the just do?
(Psalm 10: 3)

The sixteenth century brought about the most profound and far-reaching change in the position, role and identity of the secular priesthood in Christian history. The impact of the religious, social and political upheaval at the Reformation changed beyond recognition how priests were able to function, and the context and culture within which they did so. That change, and the response to it, created not only new responsibilities and tasks, but a new way of living and being amongst Christian people.

In England and Wales the upheaval was prolonged and confusing, with elements of compromise, adaptation and internal conflict. It is not surprising that what happened in England and Wales through the sixteenth century has been described in the plural, as 'English Reformations'.[8] Nothing before or since has compared with the uncertainty inflicted on the priest, on his training and way of life, on his relationships with fellow clergy and with the laity, on the authority exercised by him and over him, on his legal and political position and on his public role in society.

Generally, early sixteenth century English lay people valued the pastoral care and sacramental ministry of the priests in their midst, even if they grumbled at the costs.[9] Early Protestant and Humanist writers criticised the alleged ignorance of the parish clergy, but this was not widely taken up by parishioners.

> People wanted virtuous and honest priests to say Masses for their souls, not skilled and learned graduates; it was lasciviousness and drunkenness, and idleness that aroused the wrath of parishioners, not educational mediocrity.[10]

As long as priests continued to have a unique share in the sacred, to which they gave ordinary people access, they were valued, or, at worst, grudgingly tolerated. 'The visitation returns of the diocese (of Lincoln) suggest that they either found little to complain about in their pastor, or they were sufficiently sympathetic to his offences to connive at them.'[11] If people understood nothing else about the Mass, they knew that it made Christ present among them, and for this they depended upon the agency of the priest.

Lay Catholics, whilst conscious that not all priests were of the highest moral or intellectual calibre, recognised their dependence on his sacramental ministry. The incongruity between ideal and reality was a source of disquiet, but not, in England, a provocation for widespread anticlericalism. Personal and parochial disputes did become more common in the early sixteenth century, as the avoidance of tithes, the tax paid directly to the parish priest, grew commonplace. If the clergy clung to their status, rights and privileges, and therefore insisted on extracting every last penny of their taxes and fees, there was likely to be trouble.[12]

The quality of priests was a matter for debate, but the quantity of clergy was a looming problem. There were probably around 20-25,000 priests in England and Wales in the first decades of the sixteenth century. Evidence suggests that ordinations steadily increased from the middle of the fifteenth century, followed by a largely unexplained decline from the 1520s onwards.[13] In the huge diocese of Lincoln, stretching from the Humber to the Thames, the drop in ordinations from 141 in 1522-1527, to 80 in 1527-1535, and to only 22 between 1536 and the end of Henry VIII's reign in 1547 is remarkable.[14] A similar slump was noted in endowments to chantries and colleges, and in lay bequests to individual clergy, which went into rapid and terminal decline. All of this hints at something of a crisis in the secular priesthood, and in the traditional mutuality of the relationship between the clergy and laity.

The challenge posed to the priesthood in the sixteenth century was more than a response to late medieval grumbles, but a complete realignment with its roots, brought on by fundamental theological and cultural shifts. The issue would be, the extent to which those fundamental shifts would convince everyone. Whilst principled Protestantism remained a minority position, theological concepts of priestly ministry did become the subject of fierce debate in England. Protestant ideas of clerical functions, emphasizing the need for a 'Godly preacher' contrasted with the traditional Catholic sacramental identity.

The transformation of the sacramental priest into the Protestant preacher was, however, a long, slow and contradictory process. Protestants looked for a radical redefinition of the clerical role, so the emphasis began to shift to the personal ideals of holiness and morality of life, and the professional skills required of a minister. This redefinition led to a fundamental change, not only in the social or even religious functions of the priest, but in what his role was in society, and who he was.

The Reformation Parliament between 1529 and 1536 began to undermine the social and economic position of the clergy, hitting clerical pockets, and fueling more generalized murmuring against the inadequacies and failings of priests. By then, the discrediting of priests and the reduction of their financial independence in the community was a useful adjunct to theological demands for the eradication of the sacrifice of the Mass and the abolition of sacraments. The clergy formally submitted to the Henrician reforms on 15th May 1532, and on the following day, Thomas More resigned his position as Lord Chancellor. By the end of the year, he had produced his *Apology*, containing his most trenchant defence of the independence of the clergy.[15]

The increasingly Protestant direction of worship and practice meant that the sacrament of confession, which had been central to traditional priestly sacramental identity and, therefore, to the relationship between priest and people, waned in frequency and popularity. Where it survived, there was a greater emphasis on the personal qualities of a confessor, rather than on the inherent sacramental power of the priest.[16] The decline of individual confession marked a fundamental breach in the centuries-old relationship between people and their parish priest. Chaucer's parson was under threat as never before. For the laity, it represented freedom from a dependent, frequently uncomfortable closeness, but also the loss of the irreplaceable intimacy, familiarity, human wisdom and understanding.

Life for the secular clergy became more difficult as they endured the loss of status and credibility, and the gradual process of disengagement between priest and people. The traditional assumptions about clerical life were disappearing. The future was unclear, and clergy were receiving conflicting signals about the direction and extent of reform, as court, government and country were divided. Reform varied widely in its scope and severity, and all over the country, in the 1540s, there were unreformed or half-reformed service books. Plenty of clergy resisted the changes introduced by the reformers, and plenty of laity objected to the loss of holydays and the abolition of traditional and beloved religious practices, such as pilgrimages, processions, devotions to the saints, relics and shrines. Despite resistance, the extent to which the world was being turned upside down could not be masked.

Protestant worship was firstly permitted, and then from 1547, under Edward VI, made mandatory, and confiscation of Church property gathered pace. Most parishes acquiesced in listing items for confiscation, and by the end of 1550 the clearance was comprehensive in the Midlands and North. Pillaging of churches became commonplace and most stone altars had been removed.[17] What was under way was the destruction of the sacred and social space in which priest and laity had, for generations, found their meeting point. The parish church no longer represented the faith of generations of families who had built pulpits and roodscreens, donated statues and altars and commemorated their forebears in brass, silver, gold and stone. It meant, literally and metaphorically, the sale of the family inheritance.

Priesthood and its meaning were no longer universally accepted or understood. The reconfiguration of the role and function of the priest was one of the most tangible manifestations of the doctrinal change to Protestantism, made evident in the exchange of tabernacle and altar for pulpit and table, Latin for vernacular and celibacy for marriage.[18] The chancel and altar, the privileged space of the priest who offered the sacrifice of the Mass, were ripped out of his hands, and given over to lay patrons and Godly preachers. For any priests unable to reconcile their conscience with the reforms, those spaces would never again be accessible, and the remnant of the sacramental priesthood would be forced to survive for generations without settled sacred spaces, altars and consecrated vessels to call their own.

Permitting clerical marriage was part of the redefinition of the clerical state, away from a sacrificing priesthood towards a Godly and moral preacher of the Word, and a model of Christian family life.[19] Legislation in Edward VI's reign brought an end in England to the Church's insistence on clerical celibacy, in place since the eleventh century. This represented one of the most fundamental changes in the nature of the clerical profession, in the relationship between clergy and laity, and in the identity of the priest. In practice, there was a good deal of opposition to clerical marriage, and broadsheet allegations that only women of ill repute would marry a priest accompanied reports of violence between clergy wives and other women.[20] 'Dogmatic certainties were few and far between in the middle decades of the century, and the married ministry was far from being an established feature of the institutional church'.[21]

The reversal of religion under the Catholic Mary I in 1553, brought about an immediate campaign to restore altars, vestments, plate and all that was necessary for the celebration of Mass and other sacraments. Many of the items hidden to avoid confiscation, or lodged with sympathisers, came into the daylight again.[22] Mary I, together with her Archbishop of Canterbury and Papal Legate, Reginald Pole, set about a renewal of the clergy, through episcopal appointments and educational and financial reform, working with those clerics who had continued to defend the old ways and the unity of the Church. They intended to build an educated, resident, preaching, pastoral body of priests, who would renew the Church in England and Wales. The abolition of clerical marriage and reinstatement of celibacy was a priority. Royal injunctions swiftly set out a process for the disciplining of clergy who had married, giving authority to bishops to remove them from office, although clemency was allowed to those now widowed, or prepared to live a celibate life.

Mary inherited sixteen bishops from her father or brother, but she and Pole appointed twenty more, overwhelmingly university theologians with a proven pastoral track record and a reputation for Catholic loyalty.[23] Many were remarkable, pastoral, energetic men, sharing a Catholic, Humanist inspired vision with Pole, and keen to enact his reforming ideas. They co-operated with Pole in the Synod of Westminster in 1555, at which he put forward his new idea of seminaries to train priests under the oversight of bishops. This was a short lived experiment in England, but Pole's real triumph was posthumous, when the Council of Trent, in 1563, adopted his seminary scheme across the whole Church.

The deaths of Mary I and Pole within hours of each other, in November 1558, presented the ultimate dilemma for bishops and priests. There was now a generation of priests who had been ordained to celebrate Mass in the 1530s and 1540s, may have married and acquiesced in Protestant forms of worship under Edward VI, or been deprived of office and imprisoned, and put their wives away and rescued their hidden vestments in the 1550s. Those priests who had, with greater or lesser enthusiasm, become part of the Marian Catholic revival now found themselves facing yet more upheaval.

A Time of Uncertainty

I have no means of escape, not one who
cares for my soul.
(Psalm 142: 4)

Following Elizabeth I's accession, the Act of Uniformity and Oath of Supremacy were swiftly reinstated, with a legal obligation on the laity to attend services according to the Book of Common Prayer in the Established Church. Uniformity was imposed by the law, and the position of the clergy was made clear:

> And that if any manner of parson, vicar, or other whatsoever minister...refuse to use the said common prayers, or to minister the sacraments in such cathedral or parish church...or shall wilfully or obstinately standing in the same, use any other rite, ceremony, order, form, or manner of celebrating of the Lord's Supper, openly or privily, or Matins, Evensong, administration of the sacraments, or other open prayers, than is mentioned and set forth in the said book...or shall preach, declare, or speak anything in the derogation or depraving of the said book, or anything therein contained, or of any part thereof, and shall be thereof lawfully convicted...shall lose and forfeit to the queen's highness, her heirs and successors, for his first offence, the profit of all his spiritual benefices or promotions coming or arising in one whole year next after

his conviction; and also that the person so convicted shall for the same offence suffer imprisonment by the space of six months.

A second offence incurred a year's imprisonment, and a third offence, life imprisonment.[24] There was now a legal distinction between clergy who accepted the Elizabethan Settlement and conformed, and those who refused. Priests who refused to conform became outlaws, and faced a stark choice between acquiescence, prison or flight into exile. Catholic life and worship in England faced the real possibility of extinction.

For those who were reluctant to conform, the immediate issue was how to exist as a Catholic priest and exercise a sacramental ministry among people who might seek it. Even more fundamentally, how were they to find those who sought that ministry, without risking life and limb? Their medieval forebears had never had to seek out penitents or communicants, couples ready to marry or those close to death, for they lived in their midst. If a farm worker, ale house keeper, maidservant or merchant wished to receive the sacraments according to the rites of the Catholic Church after 1558, there was a real, practical difficulty in bringing priest and people together.

The church building and its adjoining house in the villages and towns of England and Wales no longer promised the sacramental ritual familiar to those brought up in the last decade of Henry VIII's reign, or who had glimpsed it in Mary's brief five year reign. The social, emotional and economic pressure, as well as the religious confusion, was immense. Faced with the reality of never again worshipping alongside friends and neighbours, or of entering the church in which he had baptised, married and buried the people with whom he had lived, the prospect for the priest was bleak.[25]

A priest who refused to conform lost his home, his church, his livelihood and access to the people with whom he had been brought up, and to whom he had ministered. Surveying the scene around him in 1560, he could not have been anything other than terrified. This degree of dislocation seemed to presage destruction, yet it was not entirely hopeless. What it called for was the courage to create a new and radically different way of life. The secular priests of the 1560s and 1570s were faced with the choice between creating something new, or avoiding it by compromise and conformity to the world around. They had to face the assault on the familiar and ask new questions, recognising that what was possible in the past was not so any longer, nor would it necessarily be so in the future.

To those who sought to find ways of not conforming to the Elizabethan Settlement, loyalty to the unity of the Church, a celibate sacramental priesthood and the sacrifice of the Mass went hand in hand. They faced a world in which a combination of courage, circumspection, flexibility and compromise would be needed, and in which their capacity to think beyond the unthinkable and behave in unfamiliar ways would be tested.

The surviving Marian bishops and the majority of senior clergy refused to take the Oath of Supremacy. Most of the parochial clergy, however, seem to have conformed in some fashion. As Eamon Duffy reflected, Sir Christopher Trychay was an example of 'one of the most puzzling aspects of Tudor religious history, the conformity of the overwhelming majority of clergy, despite their conservative opinions'.[26] The Mass and the other sacraments had been rejected by the newly established Church, the law, the court and parliament, and gradually by the majority of the population. So had priestly celibacy, with married clergy gradually becoming an established feature; by 1570, the debate had fizzled out.[27]

The 1560s and 1570s were a transitional phase, in which official Protestantism made little real progress, and uncertainty over the future of English religion was commonplace. There was a blurring of distinctions rather than a clear cut divide into Catholic and Protestant, and there is substantial credible evidence of the survival of traditional religion. Priests and laity tried to work out what level of compromise with the new religious settlement was compatible with their faith in the universal Church, the authority of the Pope, and a sacramentally ordained priesthood.

The practice of 'occasional conformity' grew up among those lay people who wanted to stay within the law, whilst continuing to attend Mass and the sacraments. It was forbidden by the Pope in 1562, and in the following year a Royal Commission was set up to enforce the Oath of Supremacy and attendance at the Established Church. In most parishes, the enforcement of the Act seems to have encountered acquiescence or co-operation.[28]

There were, however, those lay people and priests who hoped for yet further change in their lifetimes, and hid away vestments, books, statues and altar plate in the hope of a return to Catholic worship.[29] A change of monarch and a restoration of Catholicism were by no means impossible. No-one knew how long Elizabeth would live, and the last two quick changes in succession had brought about a change of religion.

England had no new priests ordained using the Catholic rite, but substantial numbers survived from Mary's reign. As late as the 1590s there were still as many as forty or fifty of them alive.[30] The evidence of the life and work of the men determined to continue as Catholic priests, serving those lay people who wished to retain the old ways, is difficult to obtain and to interpret. Their lives were hidden and secretive. They faced official harassment, social exclusion, loss of home and employment, and ultimately, imprisonment. Some conformed, and later returned to Catholic rites, others resisted conformity for years, before finally falling into line. Others combined minimal conformity with continued celebration of the sacraments, as long as suspicious neighbours or officious magistrates did not come snooping.

This was a time of confusion and uncertainty, requiring conviction, courage and imagination on the part of priests who found themselves all too easily on the wrong side of the law. The fundamental question facing priests in Elizabethan England was how, if at all, they could envisage the continuity of Catholicism. Mortality would eventually put paid to the survivors of the Marian Church, and the new regime could afford, for the time being, to enforce the new religious settlement and wait for the inevitable. It proved not to be so simple.

The surviving Marian priests maintained a fragile Catholic presence and a sacramental priesthood, but also laid important foundations. Exile to Catholic Europe, for those priests unable to conform or reluctant to compromise, presented one solution, with the possibility of regrouping, ready for a change of monarch or at least a modification of policy. It also presented the glimmer of an inventive solution. Under Mary, the universities, particularly Oxford, had undergone a short-lived resurgence. Mary had enthusiastically supported Catholic scholars at Oxford, where she founded Trinity and St John's Colleges. Almost every head of college was deprived of office on Elizabeth's accession, and it was the dons from Oxford who would form the first network of English priest-scholars in continental Europe.

The medieval university town of Leuven (Louvain) in the Spanish Netherlands (modern Belgium) provided the first centre for Catholic exiles. Leuven was geographically accessible, and under Catholic Spanish rule, and two houses of English priests, named Oxford and Cambridge by the men who fled from England's ancient universities, were established there.

This was not, at first, a co-ordinated scheme, but an instinctive response, which would, in time, be developed by visionary leaders into a life-saving enterprise. For some, exile offered what they hoped would be a temporary refuge, for others a deliberate choice of a new life in Catholic Europe, and for a few, a launch pad for the campaign to reclaim Catholic England. For the first time, it became necessary for leadership to be exercised by those with the vision, capacity and determination, rather than those who held office. The English clergy could not wait for the few remaining exiled bishops to secure the survival and continuity of priesthood outside the shelter of the Established Church.

A Missionary Life

When Jesus Christ is revealed, your faith will have been tested and proved like gold.

(1 Peter 1: 6-9)

Among the exiled communities, other residences took root. A college was founded in Douai (now in northern France), also under friendly Spanish control, as a refuge for scholars and clerical leaders who would be needed when the longed-for restoration of Catholicism occurred in England, preferably as a result of a change of monarch. Slowly, Douai grew from a scholarly refuge to something resembling the training centres for priests envisaged by the Council of Trent in 1563, when it adopted Reginald Pole's idea of seminaries. Exiled Englishmen realised that if they failed to make provision for successors to the small number of ageing Marian priests, Catholicism in England was finished. There was no possibility of clerical formation in England, either in the traditional medieval style, or in the newly minted Tridentine seminary form.

The English College in Douai, founded by the exiled Oxford don William Allen, was officially opened on 29th September 1568, and the first few priests trained there arrived in England in 1574.

> The first seminary priests and their Jesuit colleagues represented one of the most effective experiments of an exceptionally innovative and turbulent period of Christian history, and it was Allen's vision that they incarnated. No English Protestant attempt to rethink ministry, or to equip

men for ministry, was half so radical, or so professional. No one else in that age conceived so exalted nor so demanding a role for the secular priesthood, and no one else apart from the great religious founders produced a body of men who rose to that ideal so eagerly, and at such cost.[31]

The college was forced by changed political circumstances to move to Rheims from 1578 until 1593. Return to Douai then became possible, where the college remained until its suppression during the French Revolution at the end of the eighteenth century. Allen became, until his death in 1594, the *de facto* leader of English Catholicism, although he never saw his homeland again.[32] Douai was the foundation for further colleges for the formation of secular priests, in Rome in 1579, Valladolid in 1589 and Seville in 1592, both in Spain, and Lisbon in 1622. They began the creation of a new kind of Catholic secular priest in England – the missionary.

The vocabulary of mission entered the language of priestly identity. In the clash of cultures between the newly secure Elizabethan establishment and Catholic determination to survive, the task of the exiles was mission. Every priest ordained in one of the overseas colleges took what became known as the missionary oath, promising to serve the Catholic community in England, if necessary at the cost of his life.[33]

This newly reshaped secular priesthood did not necessarily represent either a break with the past, nor the launch of the Counter-Reformation in England. The college at Douai and those founded from it were influenced less by the Council of Trent than by William Allen's leadership and his understanding of the needs of English Catholicism. As Elizabeth's reign became more secure, and she survived plots and subterfuge, ruthlessly destroying her enemies, a successful Catholic coup to replace her became less likely. In Elizabeth's England, it was crucial to maintain the possibility of Catholic life and practice among those willing and able, by producing priests.

That missionary character has never deserted the English secular priesthood, and is embedded in its very identity. The missionary priests became the foundation stones of Catholic survival and renewal in this country, on which its new structures would stand. They continually had to reshape themselves in the changed circumstances of Catholic life, but remained conscious of their missionary identity. The first widely available account of the martyrs of the Reformation, was published by Richard Challoner in 1742, under the title, *Memoirs of Missionary Priests*, even though it also contained some accounts of lay martyrs.[34] As late as the nineteenth century, the lists of secular clergy in the Catholic Directories for England and Wales were headed 'Missionary Priests'. More recent generations have preferred the term 'pastoral priest', as coined by Cardinal Manning in the 1880s, although 'diocesan priest' has become common usage in the last century or so. These terms all reflect something about the history and identity of the priests who form the majority of parish clergy.

The concept of mission took on a very particular meaning in England and Wales. A rhetoric of missionary fervour built up courage, but there was a difference between the rhetoric and the reality of priestly life. William Allen, in Douai, came to recognise that the objective of the English mission had to be more pastoral than evangelical. A distinction was drawn between conversion from outright Protestantism and reconciliation of fearful or timid Catholics. What was vital, and, even more importantly achievable, was the rescue of waverers. The challenge lay in stiffening the resolve of the remaining Catholics who were under religious, social and economic pressure.

Reaching those who might be susceptible, rather than confronting outright opponents, was likely to be more fruitful and less dangerous. The newly ordained were specifically instructed about rallying existing pockets of Catholicism, and transforming careless Catholics into conscientious and courageous witnesses. Allen was well aware that too rigid an approach would drive people away, and he urged priests to be gentle and balanced in their approach, while maintaining Church discipline. Successful reclamation called for a 'subtle and supple approach'.[35] It was a mission based on realism and pragmatism, which came to be deeply characteristic of the forms of English Catholicism that emerged in later generations.

As the Elizabethan government became more nervous in the light of renewed threats of plots, treason and possible invasion, waiting for mortality to bring Catholicism to an end was no longer an option. It was not prepared to countenance the continued presence of the new Catholic priests who seemed to pose a perpetual threat. In 1585, the Act Against Jesuits and Seminary Priests reinforced the old legislation, and made it a criminal act to be a priest within Elizabeth's realm. A seminary priest was legally defined as one ordained outside the Queen's dominions by the authority of the See of Rome at any date after 24th June 1559, and he was regarded as a traitor:

> It shall not be lawful for any Jesuit, seminary priest, or other such priest, deacon, or religious or ecclesiastical person whatsoever, being born within this realm...made, ordained, or professed, or hereafter to be made, ordained, or professed, by any authority or jurisdiction derived, challenged, or pretended from the see of Rome...to come into, be, or remain in any part of this realm...and if he do, then every such offence shall be taken and adjudged to be high treason; and every person so offending shall for his offence be adjudged a traitor.[36]

The mood had changed, and confrontation between faith and country was inevitable. From the 1580s onwards, the language of priesthood was freighted with even more intense meaning. The seminary priest, as defined by statute, was an outlaw and a traitor in the land of his birth, purely by virtue of his ordination, and subject to grotesque violence at the hands of the state. Far from the centre of the intimate network of relationships that characterised medieval society, he was a man alone, in fear of his life, not for what he did, but for who he was. The term 'seminary priest', first coined by a hostile government, became something of a badge of honour among later generations of priests, who associated themselves with the men of the sixteenth and seventeenth centuries whose priesthood had cost them their lives.

Seminary priests were trained with death in mind, and introduced to the horrors of martyrdom by graphic illustrations such as the frescoes in the English College, Rome.[37] Places where priests were executed became substitutes for the destroyed shrines of medieval Catholicism. They could be places of 'ideological resistance and theatrical conversionary potential', and a means of participation in an event that increasingly defined Catholic faith and identity.[38] Prisons also took on a strange new significance. Where gaolers were sympathetic, bribable or merely careless and lazy, prisons could provide a haven for Catholic networks and the exchange of information, support, and sacramental life. There was a twist in the fact that it was the traditional comforter, the priest, who was now the prisoner and the victim.[39] The accounts of priestly martyrdom were cherished as much by the laity as by other priests, and took on powerful meaning in the sustenance of Catholic life.

> The stories of priestly martyrdom set out the essential truths of Tridentine Catholicism, with an emphasis on Eucharistic elements of martyrdom and privileged status of priesthood. The priest is clearly described in language echoing that of the Passion, and transformed into the imitation of Christ. The martyr story became a re-enactment of Calvary.[40]

The contrast between the role of missionaries in their hostile homeland and the pre-Reformation status and role of parish clergy was dispiriting for Elizabethan secular clergy, some of whom never emerged from nostalgia for the old ways, and the hope of a Catholic monarch to return England to the shelter of the Church. As the structures that had sustained medieval religion were stripped away, the maintenance of Catholic life constantly needed fresh impetus. The priests of the Elizabethan generation had to embark on a perilous journey of loss and rediscovery. Patterns of survival varied, as Catholics found different ways of living with limited resources, scattered congregations, few priests and little institutional life.

Conscience and Compromise

May your hand be on the man you have chosen, the man you have given your strength.

(Psalm 79: 18)

Catholicism in England and Wales was forced to make a slow and painful transition from Christian culture to denominational identity. The recognition gradually spread that a Catholic restoration was becoming increasingly unlikely, and tolerated minority status was the best that could be hoped for. It was not reached without painful internal dissension between those who continued to insist that the ultimate goal was a change of monarch and of national religion, and those who took a more pragmatic route, arguing that it was both possible and desirable to be faithful to the Pope and the Church, as well as loyal to a Protestant monarch.

The mission of the seminary priests succeeded in creating a Catholicism that would survive, although, arguably, it did not maximise the potential size and distribution of a Catholic minority community.[41] This was because there was no overall strategic plan for the deployment of seminary priests once they arrived on English soil. The priests were to be found, not always where pockets of continuity could be identified, but where it was safe for them to live and minister. Safety ensured continuity, but it did not encourage boldness of action.

The solution to the practical difficulties lay not with the priests themselves, but with the laity. The enforced homelessness of priests and the fragmented nature of Catholic congregations meant that the laity became crucial in the emergence of independent local action. Where family instincts and tradition leaned towards Catholic practice, and to papal rather than royal authority over religion, a gentry or aristocratic household could become the key to Catholic survival. The households of the gentry and aristocracy offered protection for the priest and for those in need of his ministry. They also preserved the faith of the social, political and economic leaders who had remained Catholic, and who, therefore, had the potential to secure the future. Land, wealth and political power put them in a position, when the time was ripe, to achieve political freedom and toleration. If they were lost, then the mission would be thinly spread and even more risky, serving only those with little capacity to influence their own future or that of the wider community.

The new creation that arose was a remarkable network of association and mutual reliance between the seminary priests and the laity. It rebuilt Catholic life, based on the ancient traditions of interdependence and intimacy. As in medieval society, the laity held the purse strings, while recognising their need of the priests' sacramental ministry, but Recusant Catholicism built different patterns of behaviour between priests and laity. The new dimension was the absence of ecclesiastical structures and clerical leadership, combined with the dangerous legal position of priests. Leadership in a hostile environment had to depend on informal networks.

The Catholics who went about their daily lives in an indifferent and often dangerous world had no option but to adapt flexibly to the reality of fewer priests. A form of organisation gradually emerged, with safe houses and circuits set up to receive priests and enable the sacraments to be celebrated. Some Recusant houses had a continuous clerical presence, where Mass was regularly celebrated, but this was by no means universal, and the travelling missioner was more common than the settled chaplain. Other houses were used as distribution centres for clergy and places of respite, where 'young priests could wait while postings were found for them, and older ones could meet for conferences and retreats and rest between fatiguing and nerve-wracking journeys, often on foot, to remote villages and farmhouses'.[42]

Ancestry and kinship were central to these complex networks, and became important in the deepening sense of Catholic identity among the Recusant gentry. Increasingly, Catholics in England and Wales believed that it was in the family that faith should be propagated, and family persuasion was often effective in convincing wavering Catholics. This influenced the shape that the Recusant Catholic community took, and how it lived out its beliefs.

The pattern of life that developed was based on the protection and hospitality of Catholic gentry and aristocracy extended to seminary priests. It was typically a life of secrecy and dissembling for all involved. Women maintained the domestic Recusant communities and nurtured the faith of families, often exercising effective and covert leadership. They ran the discreet households in which priests were sheltered and protected, making life and death decisions about the trustworthiness of servants and workmen, and even facing armed pursuivants and denying them the access that meant capture for a hidden priest.

Few priests had much in the way of personal resources, and relied on stipends or gifts from the laity, so inevitably appointments to a household could be a source of dispute between religious superiors, gentry patrons and individual priests. The social status of the priest in the household was problematic; he might be treated as a servant, or as a family member, or something in between, such as a tutor. Arguments between patron and priest, often over the extent to which the patron was willing for his house to be used as a base for a wider mission, possibly compromising his privacy and security, were far from rare.

The shadowy history of the individual secular priest is central to understanding the reshaping of priestly identity that took place in this period. This historical experience left little record, so evidence for its influence is difficult to produce, but reflection on what it meant in the lives of individuals and how it shaped generations of priests is worthwhile. The habit of independent, self-determined action became automatic, accompanying the isolation in which most of them lived. This unique and formative experience lasted through generations, for over two hundred years, and became part of the way in which secular priests saw themselves. It became fundamental to the identity of the secular priesthood in England and Wales, which was shaped by the historical context in which priests operated for centuries.

The element of priestly life, which is recorded in the trial accounts in State Papers, but of which it is impossible to know the personal impact, was secrecy. Clergy and laity were forced to use concealment, pretence, aliases, forgery, disguises, and hiding places. The clergy in particular, had to be prepared to move quickly and secretly, to respond circumspectly to prying questions, and use all means to avoid arrest and torture. Priests were regarded as criminals, and had to behave like criminals in order to survive, not just for themselves, but for the sake of others. This longstanding pattern of life had a pervasive effect on Catholic mentality, creating a 'collective, if partly unconscious, self-perception of criminality and also giving rise to internally legitimated mendacity'.[43]

Mullett raised questions about how this lifelong pattern of behaviour affected priests' personal and priestly integrity, about how such dissembling was reconciled with the ideal of priesthood, and to what extent it fuelled the hostile Protestant image of Catholic priests as duplicitous and dishonest.[44] All of these questions were an additional burden for the consciences of the seminary priests, who often had to make moral decisions without guidance or support.

Conscience was also an element in their dealings with the lay people on whom they depended for survival. Many of the Catholics that priests encountered were in situations which required compromise between faith and the law. Survival often depended on compromise. Meeting these cases of conscience, and dealing with the pastoral complexities involved, produced a new discipline within ecclesiastical studies, that of casuistry. The art of remaining truthful while not incriminating oneself or others, was otherwise known as 'equivocation'. The extent to which equivocation was legitimate was a source of conflict between clergy, with the secular priests generally taking a firmer line than the Jesuits.

Casuistry became an important element in English seminary formation. Priests were urged to use practical and pragmatic considerations in dealing with cases of conscience in England. 'Condoning conformable conduct, securing a measure of official pity for convinced but compromising Catholics, was a pastoral policy and practice actively sponsored by William Allen.'[45] Lay people needed guidance through the labyrinth of avoiding fines, imprisonment and execution, whilst keeping their faith. Recusant literature allowed a considerable degree of flexibility and judgement to be used by priests, aware of the difficulties faced by lay Catholics in England.[46] The language of mercy was deeply rooted in Recusant pastoral practice. 'Be assured that in most cases of this kind, the way of mercy is safer than the rigour of justice', Allen wrote in the early 1590s.[47]

A good deal of latitude was allowed to those who compromised intermittently, and it was possible for outward conformity to be given dispensation in difficult circumstances. A fine line was to be drawn between distinguishing oneself as a Catholic and taking risks unnecessarily. Life-threatening situations exempted individuals from public admission of Catholicism, and Catholic servants of Protestant masters or Catholics travelling in a mixed group were not expected to make themselves vulnerable. Infrequent and reluctant occasional conformity was often recommended for heads of household, where it could be used as camouflage for the maintenance of an underground Catholic life. Dispensations were allowed to aristocratic Catholics, where resistance would have led to loss of office, wealth and land, crucial for the reconstruction of Catholicism in the longer term.

Sacramental confession was strongly re-emphasised by the Council of Trent in 1551, but in England it was outlawed by the Elizabethan religious settlement. Catholic priests were few and far between, so the sacrament of confession gradually became less readily available to Catholics, few of whom came into regular contact with a priest. The penitential cycle, which had tied priest and people in a close bond in medieval society was largely broken.[48]

To replace it, texts were produced by priests for penitents that they would never see. They advised the laity how to confess and receive absolution without a priest, by means of making a private examination of conscience, and directing their confession to God. They were to judge their own sins and impose a penance on themselves, following the guidelines in the text. The authors assured the penitent that God would reward such efforts and purify the soul. English Catholics were being asked to alter their traditional understanding of penance, to perform it not in church, but at home in private, yet still under clerical direction.

The authors, in effect, stood in for the parish priest, and the clerical mediation happened in a different way. The majority of authors were secular priests, who were not advocating a challenge to traditional doctrine on confession, nor did they discourage approaching the sacrament if a priest was available. One of their primary concerns was to reinforce 'the Church's chain of command and the pastoral role of priests in function if not in traditional, institutional form'.[49] What emerged was a compromise between Church teaching and practice, and the difficulty faced by English Catholics maintaining their faith.

This pragmatism formed part of the framework of a new kind of interdependent relationship between clergy and laity. Evidence of the celebration of sacraments is hard to come by. The Tridentine *Rituale Romanum* was not published at all in England until 1614, and priests continued to use the pre-Reformation *Sarum Rituale*.[50] Occasional accounts have survived of elaborate celebrations of Easter and Christmas, but the liturgy depended on whether it took place in a large and wealthy house, with a settled chaplain, or in a smaller establishment offering shelter to a travelling missioner. The resources available varied accordingly. From 1615, an abbreviated missal was available, which priests could carry in their pockets, but it could still be enough to get a man arrested. In between liturgical celebrations, a steady supply of manuals, mainly imported secretly from Europe, provided the means for household or communal prayers in lieu of formal liturgy.[51]

The laity gradually developed a form of Catholic life that was often more self-reliant and domestic than communal, and the role of the priests adapted accordingly. Gatherings for Mass and the sacraments, were rare and secret, with small numbers in attendance and little in the way of solemnity, so domestic piety became the norm. Domestic piety and individual spirituality had taken root in England from the late fifteenth century, as illustrated by the ownership and usage of Books of Hours, although this was mainly limited to the wealthy and literate.[52] Some of these texts survived in secret, or were copied, allowing reprints to be smuggled into England from exiled communities in Europe. The missionary rhetoric of the seminary priests and the domestic scale of the mission produced a renewal of personal devotional and spiritual life but in different forms.

Leadership and Conflict

May you be made strong with all the strength that comes from his glorious might, so that you are able to endure everything with patience.

(Colossians 1: 11)

The possibility of missionary priests organising themselves effectively was limited by the loss of the traditional structures that had controlled the lives of the secular clergy. Training priests was one thing, but co-ordinating their activities, exercising discipline and avoiding capture in England was quite another. Priests were frequently arrested within days of landing, or even, like William Bishop, one of the first men ordained in Rome and sent to England in 1581, at the port of entry. Disguised as a merchant, when asked what his trade was, he hesitated and was arrested. Only the government's wish to avoid too many executions, to improve its relations with France, saved Bishop, and he was loaded into a boat with a number of other priests and deposited on the coast of France.[53] Survival, in large part, was a matter of luck, but co-ordination and organisation would make the odds better. It would also make better use of the available manpower, by dispersing it appropriately. Despite an agreement between secular clergy and Jesuits in 1580 to formulate a joint operation, that did not happen. The question of leadership and direction became entangled in personal and ecclesial rivalries, and conflicting political ambitions.

After the death of William Allen in September 1594, the English mission lacked any effective leadership. Serious divisions had already arisen between the Jesuits and the majority of secular priests, as they had done in other parts of Europe, particularly Holland.[54] The English secular priests wanted direct episcopal governance, along with a restoration of some of the institutional structures of the pre-Reformation church. The Jesuits and their supporters believed that the only future for English Catholicism lay in a disciplined missionary organisation under experienced Jesuit leadership. This caused resentment, not only among secular priests, but among pragmatic Recusant gentry, who had to live with the political and social realities, and preferred to keep a degree of control themselves.

This was not just a clash between the old ways and the new; in Europe the exiled secular clergy were in contact with Tridentine reformers. They particularly absorbed aspects of Church reform modelled by Charles Borromeo in his diocese of Milan, which offered an alternative version of missionary priesthood to that of the Jesuits. The Borromeo tradition had two emphases: reform by means of episcopal discipline, regulating religious orders as ancillary to the secular clergy, and reform of personal lives by strictly penitential discipline in forms later associated with Jansenism.[55] Both aspects of this tradition appealed to the English and became characteristic of the secular priests' approach to the mission.

Antagonism between seculars and Jesuits exploded at Wisbech Castle in 1594, where thirty or forty clerical prisoners were kicking their heels, until the arrival of the Jesuit leader William Weston. His attempt to enforce a code of discipline on all the imprisoned priests, secular and Jesuit alike, was the immediate trigger for fraternal discontent, but it brought other resentments to the surface. The eventual result of a campaign by 'Appellant' secular clergy in Rome was that the Jesuit and secular missions were divided. George Blackwell was appointed as the hugely unpopular archpriest of the secular clergy of England, Wales and Scotland. It proved disastrous. Blackwell's orders were to work in close consultation with the Jesuit superiors, and he was ruthless in suspending secular priests who thought he was a Jesuit stooge, and opposed his collaboration with them.

Eventually, in 1602, Pope Clement VIII revoked the instruction, instead ordering Blackwell to communicate no business to members of the Society of Jesus. This completed the institutional separation of the secular and Jesuit missions. Tempers cooled, but the secular priesthood was divided upon itself. Blackwell fell foul of both Pope and government. The Pope sacked him for urging Catholics to take a new oath of allegiance to King James I & VI, in the wake of the Gunpowder Plot. The government mistrusted his vocal support of the royal policy of religious toleration and his advocacy of obedience to the monarchy, and he died imprisoned in the Clink in Southwark, in 1613.

Agitation continued for the appointment of a bishop in England, and finally, in the 1620s, Gregory XV, who looked more favourably on the pleas of the English secular clergy, appointed William Bishop as vicar apostolic in England. Bishop forms a link in the chain connecting the Recusant secular clergy with its pre-Reformation origins. He had absorbed the tradition of Sir Thomas More, working in his family household in the 1570s. Along with More's grandson, also Thomas, he was one of the first Appellants who took the cause of the secular clergy to Rome in 1598.

More family connections with the Elizabethan secular clergy meant that the Lord Chancellor's 1530s defence of the priesthood became a point of reference for later generations of Catholics.[56] Hagiography of More was also used as propaganda to reinforce claims to Catholic continuity; in 1588, Thomas Stapleton published *Tres Thomae*, a tract which linked mission and martyrdom in witnessing to Catholic faith, in an account of St Thomas the Apostle, St Thomas Becket and Sir Thomas More.

> In the *Tres Thomae*, Stapleton, whilst fierce in his theological opposition to Protestantism, provided a carefully nuanced account of the history of the Catholic Church in England which stressed its apostolic and Roman origins. Through his deployment of martyrdom, exile and mission he offered his readers models of patience, adjustment and quiet missionary endeavour rather than those of political action and intrigue as the most effective response to what they and he saw as a persecuting regime.[57]

The distinctive identity of the post-Reformation secular clergy, rooted in its medieval origins but facing unprecedented new conditions, was beginning to emerge.

Finally, in 1623, William Bishop became the first, and much longed for, English bishop appointed since Mary I's reign. He had absorbed, as part of his French education, a 'mildly Gallican'[58] position on the independence of the local Church and limitations on papal power. Yet, whilst his appointment represented the final triumph of the Appellants, it did not have the effect of reuniting the clergy. Bishop was not what the secular clergy wanted, however good his credentials, because he only had the position of vicar apostolic and thus lacked the real authority of a diocesan bishop.

The appointment of a vicar apostolic was interpreted as emblematic of papal interference in the local Church, clerical resentment of which stretched back to the fourteenth century. Aged seventy, Bishop had a brief term in office, during which he instituted a chapter of twenty canons to advise him, and to preserve jurisdiction in the event of his death. Its appointment was recognised *de facto* in Rome, but no bull was ever promulgated to give it canonical authority, and it was a divisive and contentious element within the presbyterate for the rest of the seventeenth century.

Conflict over the question of the appointment of bishops meant that Bishop's successor, Richard Smith, was not the first choice of the English clergy. His determination to exercise full episcopal authority rather than that of a vicar apostolic, along with his lack of diplomatic skills, exacerbated divisions within the secular clergy. He continued the chapter formed by Bishop, and gave it the right to elect its own dean and canons if the vicariate was vacant, placing considerable power in the hands of this supposedly representative body of the secular clergy. Nevertheless, Smith proved unable to bend the chapter to enhance his own authority, and had the Benedictines, Jesuits, and finally many lay Catholics, openly siding against him.[59]

Suspended by Rome and threatened with arrest, Smith took refuge in France in 1631. There, he was deeply influenced by the renewal of priesthood that St Vincent de Paul was shaping, and ordained some of the priests under his direction. Inspired by St Vincent de Paul, Smith's greatest achievement was the publication of a treatise devoted to the pastoral work of the secular clergy, first published in 1630 and reissued in 1647. *Monita Quaedam Utilia Sacerdotibus Seminariis, Quando primum veniunt in Angliam:*

...ranges over the whole scope of a missioner's life, from the cultivation of an intense personal piety based on mental prayer and the sacramental life, to the conduct of chaplains towards their gentry patrons. There is guidance on matters ranging from the best means of deciding cases of conscience to details of clerical dress and diet. Preaching and individual instruction is emphasised, and significantly, there is a strong emphasis on the overriding claims of the poor on the missioner. The rulings of Trent and the obligations of the mission oath feature prominently.[60]

Smith's *Monita* also played a part in enhancing the popularity and influence in England of St Francis de Sales' *Introduction to the Devout Life*, which appealed strongly to the secular clergy, and had been available in English since 1613.[61] He appointed Thomas White, alias Blacklo, as the first English president of the newly founded English College in Lisbon in 1630. Blacklo drew up the rules for the new college, which uniquely, gave the bishop total control, making it closer than any other English college to the Tridentine model. From the first, it was intended by Smith that Lisbon should be a fully Tridentine seminary.

Blacklo became immensely influential in shaping a model of English secular priesthood, building upon Smith's *Monita* in his *Manual of Divine Considerations*. This was a course of spiritual instructions for the seminary, which included a set of meditations on priesthood and the mission, drawing on the French ideals of Pierre de Berulle and St Vincent de Paul. Blacklo left Lisbon in 1634, but the college's commitment to the ideal of a reformed priesthood, influenced by French spirituality, continued to flourish.

A published letter by Henry Gilmet, onetime procurator of Lisbon, represented 'the fullest and clearest statement of the ideals of an active secular missioner in the first half of the century'.[62] Gilmet's letter emphasized episcopal hierarchy and the secular clergy's rivalry with religious orders. He described the secular clergy as embracing all the virtues of the religious orders, and defined labour amongst the poor as the apostolic mission of the secular clergy. He listed as means to this end: voluntary poverty, obedience, sharing of spiritual resources and chastity. Other Lisbon publications followed in a similar vein, building upon Smith, Blacklo and Gilmet, including a *Liber Missionis* for students departing for

England, containing Smith's *Monita* and Gilmet's letter, to be taught to all priests before they received faculties, and a series of meditations on spiritual life, printed in 1649, including a special section on priesthood.[63]

By the middle of the seventeenth century, English secular priests were confidently articulating an approach to missionary life that absorbed theological and spiritual influences from Europe. The identity of the English secular priesthood was being forged out of a unique mixture of pragmatism, internal conflict and its own reading of Counter-Reformation spirituality. Priests were no longer engaged in short-term emergency arrangements to rescue the remnant of Catholicism, but were recognizing the need for a new approach to what was required of them to be a priest in England.

A Domestic Mission?

May he give you your heart's desire, and fulfil
every one of your plans.
(Psalm 19: 5)

Richard Smith tried to exercise episcopal jurisdiction as vicar apostolic from France, but finally resigned in 1631, undermined by continuing divisions among the secular clergy, not least within the chapter. No immediate successor was appointed, leaving the chapter regarding itself as having a free hand. The appointments of Bishop and Smith to lead the English secular clergy and oversee the mission between 1623 and 1655 were largely ineffective, leaving them still rudderless and argumentative. Blacklo's faction dominated the English chapter, and after Smith's death in 1655, he became even more powerful.

It seems that, although the secular clergy had obtained a form of governance, and a voice in their own leadership, it was impossible to find co-operation and agreement. If there was to be a new episcopal appointment, the chapter agreed that it must be a bishop who would consult with the chapter and recognise its rights, rather than a vicar apostolic, who was a direct papal appointee and could override the chapter. The Blackloists favoured government by the chapter rather than by another vicar apostolic. Other secular clergy deeply resented the power being assumed by the chapter.

This moved the whole debate about the identity of the secular clergy into a different phase. Without a bishop, within the corporate identity that the chapter was trying to create, lay the danger of leadership by a clerical clique. It also raised challenges to the existing *de facto* leadership of the Catholic community by the gentry. The archpriest controversy and the chapter battles highlighted the fact that the mission of the English secular clergy was hampered, not only by external persecution, but by lack of leadership and organization. Into this vacuum, the priests themselves entered, and competed with the religious orders and with each other for freedom, authority and even greater independence.

In 1685, the issue of episcopal governance surfaced again. To the fury of the chapter, Philip Howard OP, the Cardinal Protector of England, and the new king, James II, were of one mind in taking the question forward gently by obtaining the appointment of a vicar apostolic, not a bishop. The choice fell on John Leybourn, on condition that he took an oath not to recognise the chapter, indicating Rome's recognition that 'the clergy on the chapter were a small and not wholly representative body' and that its vision had been 'wholly inappropriate to English conditions'.[64]

What emerged as a consequence of these disputes was a form of priesthood that became increasingly self-reliant and independent in its decision-making. Each individual had to negotiate his relationship with vicars apostolic and lay patrons. This bred a culture of self-sufficiency, without the constraints of structured ecclesiastical relationships, or mutual support. It also combined, with the fragmented and geographically disparate life of the clergy, to militate against mutual co-operation, sharing of resources and fraternal support.

Howard was aware of this, and, towards the end of the seventeenth century, attempted to introduce a structured form of life into the secular priesthood in England. He advocated the adoption of the Institute of Secular Clergy, founded in Bavaria by Bartholomew Holzhauser in the 1640s. Holzhauser's scheme for a common life and mutual support among the secular clergy gained papal approval from Pope Innocent XI. Howard contemplated imposing it as a rule of life on the English College in Rome, but he also believed it would be a means of restoring morale and unity among the secular clergy already on the mission in England. In a pastoral letter of 1684 he proposed that the Institute would be a protection against clerical idleness, over-familiar contact with women and lack of control over the administration of property. This suggests that these were the problems of which he, as Cardinal Protector, was particularly conscious.[65]

The Institute was introduced to England, but membership was never large. The scheme foundered in the face of opposition from the remnants of the chapter, who saw it as a rival to its own waning influence. This was related to Howard's prolonged difficulties in relation to the chapter. A letter written by the chapter, 'To our worthy brethren of the new Institute', dealt the death blow, and it was subsequently suppressed by Bonaventure Giffard, Vicar Apostolic of the London District, in 1703.

Small groups, especially in the Midlands, resisted its abandonment. When Andrew Bromwich left his family property at Oscott, near Birmingham, for the maintenance of a priest, it was on condition that his successor was a member of the Institute. Bromwich's uncle, Daniel Fitter was a member, and took over his property and his mission. In turn, his uncle had been Henry Holden, a radical Blackloist, and Gallican, who had wanted to see the Jesuits expelled from England. While Bromwich was an Institute man, which the chapter had despised, he also represented the independence of the English secular clergy inherent in the chapter.

This was a thread that linked, by instinct as much as by blood, a fiercely independent tradition, emerging from the seventeenth century disputes. The medieval clergy were taken as a model, interference from Rome was instinctively opposed, and full episcopal government was regarded as both necessary and possible. It was profoundly inspired by the spirituality of St Vincent de Paul and St Francis de Sales, and insistent on asserting the predominance of the secular priesthood over the religious orders.

A contemporary of Bromwich at the English College, Lisbon, John Gother, was the single most influential secular priest of the eighteenth century, of whom few people have heard. He, almost single-handedly, produced the much needed English catechetical books for Recusant Catholics. Gother and Bromwich stand at the end of the period of martyrdom and the beginning of the new order of patient, hidden, methodical pastoral priesthood. Bromwich was the last English priest condemned to death for his priesthood, but the sentence was never carried out and he was eventually released.

Gother entered the English College, Lisbon in January 1668, and he remained on the staff for a decade, where he absorbed the French-inspired spirituality of the college, especially that of St Francis de Sales. He drew effectively on St Francis de Sales' spirituality of everyday life to provide his fellow priests with the tools they needed for the next phase of the mission. Gother's work 'demonstrated the secular clergy's skill in adapting to the mission after the failures of 1688',[66] and he

> represented the shift from controversy to focussing on those embattled minorities that constituted what remained of the mission...(he) demonstrated that the secular clergy had, at last, succumbed to the idea of domestic mission in a pronounced definitive manner.[67]

He 'concealed himself entirely from the world',[68] and provided the laity with simple instructions and prayers, which were published posthumously in an edition running to sixteen volumes, and included a variety of 'Instructions' for Catholics in various walks of life. By means of *Instructions for the Afflicted and Sick, Instructions for the Whole Year, Instructions for Masters, Traders, Labourers, Servants, Apprentices, Youths etc., and A Practical Catechism, Divided into Fifty-Two Lessons, for each Sunday in the Year*, the Catholic laity acquired a comprehensive spiritual guide to life.

His *Instructions and Devotions for hearing Mass* were set out in three categories: for young beginners, for the well-instructed and for the more advanced, combining catechesis with prayer. His *Instructions on Keeping the Sunday,* for Catholics who could not get to Mass, contained prayers and instructions for following the action and words of the Mass. Gother's Missal with English instructions remained in print until 1800, and was frequently reproduced through the nineteenth century. It was Gother who shaped the peculiarly English Catholic domestic piety of the eighteenth century, which emerged in the absence of opportunities for communal liturgical celebration or regular catechesis by the clergy. His work also began a movement towards the use of English, to enable greater participation by less educated people in prayer and worship. Gother's hidden achievements helped the transition from rural, gentry-based Catholicism to more urban, independent missions. Sharpened awareness of different needs provoked the secular priesthood to find new starting points and fresh modes of missionary life.

The Garden of the Soul

Make me know the way I should walk, for to you
I lift up my soul.
(Psalm 142: 8b)

From 1688 onwards, four Vicars Apostolic were nominally in authority over the English mission. This signalled 'the defeat of an independent secular clergy supported by a domestic hierarchy',[69] but their freedom of action was still hampered by lack of resources and infrastructure, and their dependence on lay patrons. For most of the eighteenth century, vicars apostolic were drawn from wealthy families who could support them and provide them with housing. Clerical life was at a low ebb. The last priests had been executed by 1680, and the focus of the more recent penal laws had been on undermining the economic and political power of the laity. This would damage the capacity and willingness of the gentry to continue to sustain the Catholic mission.

A different type of lay Catholic appeared, as the population distribution began to shift due to early industrialisation and the agricultural revolution. Urban clusters of population grew, enabling humbler people to participate in new forms of economic activity and Catholics became freer in observing their faith. A gradual easing of restrictions was experienced, although the penal laws remained on the statute book. Clerical numbers did not keep pace with the modest lay expansion. The colleges found it more difficult to recruit students, as gentry Catholicism declined. Clerical students from the first generations of Catholic 'middling classes', rarely had the means to support themselves.

The number of ordinations in the eighteenth century was considerably smaller than in the seventeenth century: 1,878 as opposed to 3,062. The largest quarterly total of ordinations across the whole period, 852, took place between 1600 and 1625. The largest number in any quarter of the eighteenth century was 525 between 1725 and 1750, with a quarterly average of around 500, but there was a marked decline between 1775 and 1800. The decline affected the religious orders as well as the secular priesthood, but the seculars were always the largest proportion, outnumbering the Jesuits by almost 2:1 over the whole period.[70]

This decline took place in the context of conflict over the running of the colleges in Douai and Rome. It was a perennial fixture for over a century, with constant complaints about the quality of priests produced by both institutions, and suspicions of Jansenism in Douai. Accusations of Jansenism were levelled at Philip Howard and at two of the first vicars apostolic, John Leybourn and Bonaventure Giffard. John Gother was one of three priests ejected in 1686 from the chapel they had built in Lime St, London, on suspicion of Jansenism, and replaced with Jesuits.

Jansenist ideas circulated widely in England, even in non-Catholic circles, and the sympathetic portrayal of a French priest in Daniel Defoe's sequel to Robinson Crusoe, *Further Adventures* was evidence of this.[71] Many English Protestants saw them as victims of papal oppression and champions of toleration, and began to appropriate Jansenist spirituality for their own use. Catholic sympathy with the rigorism and anti-papalism of Jansenists was certainly not unknown. The Jansenists' chief opponents were the Jesuits, so they were regarded as allies by some of the anti-Jesuit English secular clergy.

Complaints went to Rome, and Bonaventure Giffard had difficulty getting his fellow vicars apostolic together to coordinate a response to accusations of Jansenism within the English secular clergy. Eventually he provoked a warning from Rome to Catholics in Britain and Ireland against 'erroneous books' and persons of suspected orthodoxy, especially those who under a pretence of 'rigid morality' attacked the authority of the Holy See.[72] This was followed by a letter from the papal secretary of state to Giffard, denouncing Douai for teaching Jansenism. The vicars apostolic were finally galvanised into action, but to no great effect, and panic ensued. In September 1713, the papal bull *Unigenitus* was published, condemning Jansenism, but the sympathies of the English secular clergy were entirely with the French Cardinal Noailles, who was personally castigated.

The controversy around Jansenism was reignited in England by the publication of a moderate pro-Jansenist ruling from the Sorbonne, which became influential in Douai. The Douai authorities mounted counter measures to defend the college and the secular clergy, against charges of Jansenism. Douai was strongly associated with the Stuart royal family in exile and the Jacobite cause, and the Stuart claimant, James Edward, was greeted with great acclaim by the students when he visited Douai in 1710.[73] After the failure of the 1715 Jacobite Rising, accusations of Jansenism as well as Jacobitism were flung, and superiors in Paris and Douai saw themselves as under attack alongside their Stuart masters.[74] Catholic supporters of the Hanoverian succession wanted to isolate the colleges of France and the Low Countries from the English mission. A prolonged and bitter disputation in print ensued, creating a period of introspection and withdrawal from active involvement in university life by the college at Douai, and renewal of hostility between the Jesuits and the secular priests. This resurgence, and the replaying of old antagonisms affected the eighteenth century as much as it had done the previous one.

Douai had its own difficulties, and Lisbon was worse, but the Spanish colleges, under Jesuit direction, were in a desperate state. For a century, no students entered Madrid, and there were only a few at Seville and Valladolid. In 1740 John Talbot Stonor, the influential Vicar Apostolic of the Midland District, wanted secular clergy to take over the college in Seville and relinquish interests in Valladolid and Madrid, but the Jesuits refused. At the suppression of the Jesuits in Spain in 1767, Richard Challoner, the most senior of the vicars apostolic, persuaded the King of Spain to preserve the colleges for the training of men for England, and combine the resources of Seville and Madrid amalgamated into Valladolid. It was placed under the leadership of a secular priest for the first time. The intention was clearly to imbue Valladolid with the spirit of Douai, which was struggling itself.

In 1769, two years after the changes in Spain, Challoner petitioned Rome for a new rector for Douai. In a revealingly honest letter, he set out the college's needs, and the qualities required in a candidate, who should:

> Have a particular eye upon all that are designed for the Church or aspire that way. And be not easy in admitting such as do not give sufficient marks of a calling, by their piety

and regularity; or whose conduct is but equivocal, however they may shine as to wit or learning, and, by no means and upon no consideration, such as may be habitually addicted to any vice. Nor yet such as are incapable of attaining to necessary learning, or whose oddity of temper, or crack in the family, or behaviour, or want of common discretion disqualifies for the calling. And here I cannot but lament that greater care has not always been taken in the choices of those that have been admitted, and even sent amongst us, some of whom have wanted common sense; and that many who were sent upon funds have been suffered to continue for years after it was evident that they were unlike to come to anything, occupying the place of more hopeful subjects. Prefect, professors etc. should have an eye to this, and give timely warning or notice to superiors that such ought to be sent away without loss of time. And this you should insist upon.[75]

Dependence on the foreign colleges would continue until the 1790s, but with an increasing sense of dissatisfaction. Bitter disputes between seculars and regulars, especially Jesuits, continued to rage in a European context that would eventually result in the suppression of the Society of Jesus in 1773. The secular clergy's takeover of the Jesuit college of St Omer's, at the insistence of the French government, fuelled animosity between the seculars and Jesuits in England. Difficulties over human and financial resources and disagreements over the suitability of the formation for the needs of the mission were prevalent.

There was a growing feeling that the clergy trained abroad, often for ten or twelve years, were incapable of appreciating the needs of the English Catholic community, and that the curriculum of training was narrow, inadequate and disconnected from modern thinking. It was alleged that students developed 'a regimental community spirit marked by an intense schoolboy ritualism and traditionalism'.[76] All of these complaints ultimately found a solution, not in internal reform, but in the explosion of revolution.

Challoner became the most influential of the vicars apostolic, leading the London District from 1740 until his death in 1781. He modelled himself on Gother, and perpetuated his influence in his most famous devotional work, *The Garden of the Soul*. Challoner's own personal regime was ascetic, disciplined and regular, living in a poverty that he believed to be fundamental to the priestly life.[77] He instituted a series of weekly conferences for London priests, based on the practice established by Francis de Sales and Vincent de Paul.[78] The regulations Challoner drew up were effectively his manifesto for priestly life: daily mental prayer, annual retreat, emphasis on catechesis for children, preaching, being at home in the evenings to receive people, care for the poor and keeping out of pubs. Challoner's influence shaped priests and laity into what became known as 'Garden of the Soul' Catholics.[79]

It was Challoner who gathered together the existing evidence of the missionary priests and other martyrs, and published the first widely available account of those who had died between 1580 and 1684. Manuscript lists had been compiled since the sixteenth century, but Challoner was the first to draw them together for publication, and to attempt a comprehensive biographical history of the martyrs. The witness of the English Reformation martyrs would become part of the identity of English Catholics, and especially of the secular priesthood. The memoirs written by Challoner were the products of a Church possessed by a growing sense of stability, with an accompanying desire to take stock, to explain itself and to differentiate itself from the other varieties of English religion in the first real age of English religious pluralism.[80]

The English secular priesthood had found a very particular identity, which emphasised the independence of the English Church from papal interference, hostility to Jesuit influence and a restrained and somewhat rigorous domestic piety, shaped by Gother. This took root through the increasingly complex and fluid network of secular priests working on the English mission.

The Writing of History: Old Conflicts in New Clothes

You will lead them and plant them on your mountain,
the place, O Lord, where you have made your home.
(Exodus 15: 17)

The old issues of organisation and authority became embedded in the writing of those who began to tell the history of the Reformation, especially Charles Dodd, who was the nephew of one of the priests ejected from Lime St, a dedicated Jesuit-hater, and historian of the English College, Douai. Dodd was appointed to Harvington Hall in Worcestershire, where he spent most of his life, writing his monumental *Church History of England 1500-1688*, which played an important part in the later historiography of English Catholicism.[81] It also helped to influence the attitudes and policies of later generations of secular clergy, and keep the old disputes alive. Dodd's work 'traced the ideological dilemmas and anxieties overhanging eighteenth century Catholic life'.[82]

He idealised the pre-Reformation Church and the traditional liberties and independence of the secular clergy, describing the 'inconveniences and injustice of the Pope's pretensions', and emphatically arguing that the medieval English Church was not, as in Protestant polemic, dominated and oppressed by the papacy. He pointed out that the statutes of Edward

III had forcibly reminded the Pope of the ancient English tradition whereby 'bishops, abbots etc. should obtain their dignities by election of chapters, and that both the Popes and the Kings of England had frequently confirmed and agreed to that practice'.[83]

All the battles over the chapter and vicars apostolic were embedded in Dodd's controversial history. He stood firmly in the Blacklo tradition and defended his policies, reiterating the argument for local governance by bishops answerable to an elected chapter, with authority to keep the Jesuits and other regular clergy in check. When Dodd published his history in 1742, there was uproar within the Catholic community over his treatment of the Appellant controversy. It was vitriolic in its animosity to the Jesuits, whom he blamed for the whole sorry sequence of events. The fire was easily stoked up afresh.

> Dodd threw himself behind the old blueprint of the secular clergy, dreaming of the reconstruction of an ordered, hierarchical church, bound in oath to the laws of the kingdom, and limiting the pernicious influence of the Jesuits.[84]

The most vocal clerical spokesmen of the eighteenth century were looking for a new reading of English Catholic history, which Dodd's version gave them. It was taken up by Joseph Berington, student and professor at Douai from 1755 to 1769. Influenced by the European Enlightenment and Gallican historical methodology of his teachers at the University of Douai, Berington developed his own course of modern philosophical studies as a challenge to the whole ethos of the college. He was censured and, in 1771, dismissed from Douai, making him the hero of clerical independence.

Berington's later writings continued to express both a theological liberalism that frightened the more conservative, and a critique of what he regarded as insular and intolerant Catholicism. This form of Catholic liberalism became a fervent cause among some aristocratic laity in England and a vocal minority of clergy, including James Archer, reckoned to be the finest preacher in England, Thomas Hussey and John Bew, the secular clergy's only real theologians.

Berington's *State and Behaviour of English Catholics*, published in 1780, became the party manifesto. In it, he rewrote the history of English Catholicism, based on Blacklo and Dodd, but he also set out a wide-ranging programme of reform. He argued for 'reasonableness', universal toleration, the need for the reform of the Church through the promotion of vernacular liturgy and a change in the discipline of celibacy in the priesthood. He insisted that Catholicism was compatible with the British constitution, and that the temporal power of the papacy must be abandoned. Most startlingly, he insisted:

> Of this, however, I am convinced, that, were certain obstacles removed, such as the views of interest, the animosity of party, the blindness of prejudice, and those thick clouds which controversy has raised, it would then appear, that the Protestant Church of England and Catholics are divided by very thin partitions.[85]

In 1785 Berington was appointed to the mission founded at Oscott by Andrew Bromwich. There he made common cause with religious dissenters, including the Unitarian Joseph Priestley, and supported a public educational religious code capable of reaching all believers. One of his social circle described Berington as 'a finished gentleman of the old school, and a model of ecclesiastical decorum of the church of ancient monuments and memories',[86] but in fact, he was a man of the new era, rather than the old, who would press at boundaries on behalf of the new generation of secular clergy and laity.

Berington aligned himself with the Catholic Committee formed in 1782 and its more radical successor, the Cisalpine Club, led by Sir John Throckmorton. In 1789 the committee proposed an oath describing Catholics as 'Protesting Catholic Dissenters' in return for a measure of legal toleration. Although expressing some reservations about the oath, Berington, in 1792, placed himself at the centre of the debate between the vicars apostolic and the clergy, in support of the Cisalpine position. His 'Staffordshire Creed', *An Appeal to the Catholics of England by the Catholic Clergy of the County of Stafford*, defended the canonical rights of priests and argued that

> the Bishop of Rome (was) to be the head, supreme in Spirituals by divine appointment, supreme in discipline by ecclesiastical institution; but in the concerns of state and civil life, we believe him to be no governor, no master, no guide.[87]

This was the moment at which battle was joined anew for the identity of the English Catholic clergy. The Cisalpine school of thought held Rome at a distance, was independent of impositions by vicars apostolic, and looked more to the fourteenth century for its ecclesiastical status. On the other hand, there was an emerging vision of a disciplined and structured clerical body governed by a strong episcopate, and supported by centralized Roman spiritual and temporal authority. The group of twelve or so priests who became known as the 'Staffordshire Clergy' were in the vanguard of the Cisalpine movement. The mission at Oscott became the focus of its support, from where Berington and his circle set the tone for a process of reform in their scheme to challenge the old Douai tradition, and to finally establish seminary formation in England.

The long held dream of English seminaries would, it was hoped, address the problem of the quality and quantity of priests, by reducing the costs involved, revising the curriculum, and enhancing contact between the seminary and the mission. The transfer of seminary formation to England was rapid and sudden, with the old roots in Europe torn up as a result of the French Revolution. Colleges were destroyed, priests and students imprisoned and hasty departures made to England. Ushaw and Ware became the heirs of the Douai tradition, while the Cisalpine plans for Oscott bore fruit in a new style of educational establishment.

Education and formation on English soil began to build a stronger sense of priestly identity. Increasingly, priests became more aware of their role of leadership, and able to challenge generations of dependence on gentry patronage. They were increasingly aware of the pastoral needs of a changing, and growing Catholic population, more typically urban than rural, less likely to be financially independent, and often poorly educated. This reflected the social and economic transformation under way, as the country became industrialized.

In order to meet the changing needs, some of the clergy associated with English Cisalpinism, particularly those working in urban areas, began to advocate the use of English both in private prayer and public worship. Gother had set a pattern in private devotional and catechetical material, and English translations of the Missal were in use. Charles Cordell, an enthusiastic follower of Gother, produced a four volume *Divine Office for the Use of the Laity* in 1763. Cordell combined a manual of instruction and missal, along with vespers and compline for all Sundays, feasts and ferias, the rites of baptism, confirmation, marriage, visitation of the sick, the burial service, office of the dead, penitential psalms and litanies.

Pragmatism and adaptation to the circumstances were vital, without which, Catholic faith and practice would have dwindled, rather than being secured. Joseph Berington had no doubts about the need for vernacular forms of worship, and published *A Letter on the Use of the Latin Tongue* in which he boldly stated that part of the Mass should be celebrated in English. A number of prayer books and manuals, flowing from the Gother tradition, were published, which consisted of English prayers to augment the Mass and to enable ordinary Catholics to pray.[88] They were a product of the changing nature of the Catholic population and the emergence of Catholic public worship in towns and villages, especially after the legalisation of Catholic chapels in 1791.

The two figures who reflect most vividly the changing identity of the secular priesthood of the early nineteenth century are John Kirk and John Lingard. Almost exact contemporaries, they represent the last vestiges of an older, more independent, Cisalpine influenced, English priesthood, which looked for its roots in medieval England rather than Tridentine Europe. By the time they both died, in 1851, their ideas had largely been supplanted, but they helped to establish a deep sense of connection, and a tradition of continuity with the pre-Reformation past, within the English secular priesthood.

They both modelled something of the character of the medieval parochial clergy, spending a lifetime in a single mission, but, more influentially, their writings were imbued with that character. Kirk and Lingard, like Dodd, insisted on historical continuity between the medieval Church and their own day, using it in their defence of the rights of the secular clergy. What they sought was a future that drew on the medieval traditions of governance by local bishops, a healthy distance between Rome and England, and a diminution of Jesuit influence.

John Kirk's life spanned the establishment of the college at Oscott in the 1790s, alongside Berington, and the building of the new college in the 1830s, over which Wiseman would preside. Kirk was the last student to enter the English College, Rome under the old Jesuit regime before the suppression in 1773, a friend of Joseph Berington and a leading member of the Staffordshire Clergy. Henry Weedall, president of Oscott College, described Kirk as 'a living chronicle of persons, places and facts ... a perfect specimen of the olden times, a type of the fine old English priest; methodical, dignified, devout'.[89]

Kirk's lifelong friend, John Lingard, was the giant of this generation, both in intellectual and pastoral achievement, and in his influence on the shifting sands of English Catholic life between the age of Challoner and the age of Wiseman. At his tiny mission of Hornby, Lancashire, Lingard wrote his *History of England*, published between 1819 and 1830, and a host of smaller works of history and theology. He picked up the gauntlet of vernacular prayers and liturgy, publishing a collection of English prayers for the use of his parishioners in 1833, an English translation of the gospels in 1836, a volume of catechetical instruction in 1840, and was an early composer of vernacular hymns for congregational use.

Lingard believed that liturgy should be intelligible and attractive both to Catholic worshippers and to Protestant visitors, disliking repetitious litanies and over-fanciful metaphors. He wanted his congregation to understand and follow the priest's prayers at the altar, and in Holy Week, would have someone read the Passion narrative clearly in English while he continued quietly in Latin. Above all, he wanted simplicity, and disdained both the medievalism of the Gothic revival, and the pomp that often accompanied the opening of churches, when the church was 'turned into an opera house' with 'the bishop performing as the first dancer in the ballet'.[90]

When, in 1814, the Society of Jesus was re-established in most of Europe, Kirk and Lingard fiercely opposed any idea of reimposing Jesuit control over the English College, Rome. Leadership of the English College by secular priests reflected their determination to present Catholicism as truly English, and not as a post-Reformation import from a hostile Europe, defending untenable powers claimed by the papacy. Instead, it must be understood as the natural continuation of the medieval Church.

Lingard went to Rome himself, to prevent control of the English College falling back into the hands of the Jesuits, and to get his friend Kirk appointed as rector. Robert Gradwell was his second choice when Kirk pleaded poor health, but this appointment was, in effect, Lingard's doing. The decision to appoint a secular priest drew a line under Jesuit influence in the college after two hundred and fifty years. This was a twitch on the thread of continuity between the divisions of the sixteenth century, not only between Catholic and Protestant, but between secular clergy and Jesuits. The voices of the Appellants still echoed.

The campaign for the rights of the secular clergy took other forms. Daniel Rock was one of the last survivors of the Cisalpine tradition, and a scholar of liturgy and ecclesiastical art. He was one of the first students to enter the newly reopened English College in 1818, along with Wiseman, and a friend of the Earl of Shrewsbury, to whom he became chaplain at Alton Towers. He, like Lingard, was at pains to insert Catholic historical scholarship into the mainstream, and was one of the first modern priests who had a public role beyond the Church, being closely involved in the founding of the Victoria and Albert Museum, until his death in 1871.

An enthusiastic advocate of a restored hierarchy, Rock campaigned for it from 1840 onwards, launching a circular letter to his fellow priests – an action inconceivable a generation earlier, but a sign of growing clerical confidence. Rock framed a petition to Rome, requesting that a restored hierarchy be conditional on the priests having a voice in the election of their bishops, and demanding restrictions on the rights of bishops to move clergy between missions. Limited though the campaign was in its reach, it was a sign of newly found muscle among the secular clergy, and a determination to press for bishops who were answerable to an elected chapter. Whilst the bishops were obviously not opposed to the idea of a restored hierarchy, they were uneasy about clerical petitions and mutterings of discontent.

After the hierarchy was restored in 1850, Wiseman and the new diocesan bishops were determined to put behind them all memory of independently minded, Gallican-inspired priests. It was rumoured that Lingard had been created a cardinal *in petto* (secretly) in 1826. Wiseman, whilst acknowledging Lingard as his old teacher, did not want to disinter him as a champion of the Cisalpine tradition, and was anxious to scotch the story after Lingard's death. He ensured that a guarded obituary was published, and that no mention of the cardinalate was made in Lingard's first biography.[91] He was also determined to limit the pernicious influence of Daniel Rock, who played an incidental part in London being split into two dioceses in 1850. He was working in south London by then, and Wiseman was convinced that the worst anti-Roman clergy were to be found south of the river, and wanted nothing to do with them.

A New Kind of Missionary Priest

But I, through the greatness of your love, have access to your house.

(Psalm 5: 8)

The mood had changed, and transition was under way from the eighteenth century liberal independence of Berington to a vision of the clerical office of settled quasi-parish priests. The battleground shifted to what Bossy called 'trusteeism'[92] and the struggle for control of the direction and finance of newly founded urban missions. As gentry influence declined, and society became more urban, a new kind of Catholic lay participation emerged. The gentry patron, giving shelter and support to resident or travelling missionary priests, was supplanted by a middle class urban elite, whose local influence gave them power.

They became the builders of chapels and schools, and the patrons of the clergy who served them, often clashing with vicars apostolic over clerical appointments. Church, chapel and school building became possible as never before, with money raised from a new class of people, rather than from a single patron. England was beginning to see something resembling a Catholic middle class, but the majority of Catholics in urban and rural areas were from the poorer end of society.

The age of trusteeism was short-lived, as the vicars apostolic pressed Rome for the appointment of bishops to dioceses that reflected the spread and increase of Catholic population. Lingard, Kirk and Rock pointed the way to a new kind of missionary priest, in touch with mainstream political and cultural developments, yet also deeply concerned with the status and position of the secular priesthood. In the second half of the nineteenth century, priests built on these achievements, and began to carve out for themselves a distinctive sense of identity in the cities of Victorian England.

The post-1850 dioceses were a new creation, and belonging to one was an experience unknown to Catholic priests in England and Wales for three hundred years. This led Nicholas Wiseman, and later, Henry Edward Manning to believe that the mission was at risk in its new situation, if the aspirations of the secular clergy were not raised, by inculcating in them a love for their diocese and loyalty to their bishop, similar to that of religious for their orders.[93] Other bishops shared their concerns. In Birmingham, William Bernard Ullathorne was preoccupied with the need for priests to be properly formed, in order to fulfil their ministry effectively. The majority of his pastoral letters, over forty years of episcopal office, were concerned with seminary formation and priestly life. The whole work of a diocese, he asserted, 'depends upon the number and character of its clergy, which again, depends upon their long and effective training'.[94]

Another was Alexander Goss, Bishop of Liverpool from 1856 to 1872, who had strong views on clerical lifestyle, abhorring absence from home, dining out and love of society, 'marks of an inconstant and frivolous mind, that neither loves study nor the duties of the sacred ministry'. He found difficulties in situations where a number of priests lived together, of junior clergy challenging the authority of the missionary rector, and he reached a point where he set up a commission to establish regulations for the proper running of presbyteries.[95] Although bishop of the most Irish of dioceses, Goss was more concerned about the quality than the quantity of priests, and was determined to build up an English priesthood, and not just place Irish priests in Irish areas.[96]

Episcopal authority was a preoccupation of the bishops after 1850, particularly in the exercise of control over the seminaries on English soil. The members of the new hierarchy relished their new status, and the freedom to be independent of refugee colleges abroad, run by men over whom they had little authority. Seminaries in England could, at last, come under direct episcopal control, and there were a number of attempts at starting diocesan seminaries, which foundered for lack of resources. This fuelled disputes between bishops over the governance of the existing seminaries.

Ushaw retained in large measure the Douai tradition of independence from episcopal control, and Oscott resisted encroachment from bishops beyond Birmingham. The battle over control of Ushaw led to it being declared, by Wiseman, not a seminary in the true Tridentine sense, but Oscott went more in the direction of the Tridentine model, as Ullathorne fiercely opposed his episcopal neighbours. Finally, as the result of battles played out at the third Synod of Westminster in 1859, Rome decreed, in 1863, that control of Ushaw, Oscott and Ware lay in the hands of the diocesan bishop in whose territory they sat.

Bishops were divided on governance, but there was a measure of agreement that seminary formation, following the Tridentine model, should be entirely separated from lay education. Bishops and seminary staff complained of the 'worldliness' introduced by the lay boys, and of its damaging effects on the seminarians. The policy of separation was not universally applauded by the laity, on the quite legitimate basis that much good had flowed from shared education between laity and clergy. The benefits of more concentrated seminary formation in a quasi-monastic community, had to be balanced against the loss of shared experience and understanding among the clergy and laity who would lead the Church in the future.

There were no established parish boundaries, which often created fraternal disputes, and until 1918 the priests technically remained missionary rectors, not parish priests. The missionary rectors became the lynchpin of the revival of Catholic structures, building churches, supporting convents, organising and overseeing schools, as well as founding societies, clubs and sodalities for charitable and social purposes. The priest as builder, fundraiser and entrepreneur, was born in the second half of the nineteenth century. Less dependent on the largesse of the wealthy, missionary rectors called upon smaller contributions from an expanding industrial population, raising money wherever and however they could. They were part of a new Catholic culture emerging in England, in which the priests played an increasingly dominant role.

The beginnings of a new order were in place. The role of the priest was transformed by the practical exercise of clerical leadership and authority within the increasingly complex quasi-parochial pattern of Victorian Catholic life. Priests were increasingly striving for control, working more closely alongside the newly emergent lay leadership of local business and professional people. They made huge investments of energy in catechesis, charity schools, prayer services, confessions, lectures, fundraising events and public meetings, involving themselves in all sorts of projects within and beyond the Catholic community. A new kind of priest was emerging from the English seminaries to serve a new kind of congregation. The rebuilding of Catholic institutions, in the context of an indifferent or hostile society, transformed priests into visible public figures.

The establishment and direction of Catholic schools, in order to secure the faith of future generations, was the most valuable project of all. In particular, the priest was responsible for monitoring school attendance and for religious instruction. He was expected to spend a considerable amount of time in the schools, which were effectively part of his parochial responsibility. The language used makes clear the nature of the new relationship between priest and laity:

> The priest is the natural manager of the school, and cannot cease to be so without imminent peril of disastrous consequences. With him will rest the choice of lay associates whom he may wish to connect with himself. For there can be no desire to exclude the laity, but rather to encourage them in every possible way…to assist the clergy with their time and means. Still the priest will remain the permanent acknowledged centre of all educational efforts within his parish.[97]

This relationship was 'regularly and frequently reiterated by bishops', and in 1869, *The Tablet* asserted that the priest was the real schoolmaster, and however effective and qualified, the teacher must play second fiddle. 'If he is sharing in the priest's work, it is as the priest's instrument. He is not the great man, and can never become so; his pupils and their parents know it, and he feels it and is made to feel it.'[98]

What became known as the 'Catholic Revival' of the nineteenth century was shaped by a Catholic identity increasingly distinctive from the rest of Victorian society, and determined largely by the clergy. Led by the more confident and assertive 'Missionary Priests' listed in the Catholic Directories, the Catholic community created a counter culture around its quasi-parishes, schools, convents, charities and societies. Its extraordinary success as a missionary enterprise is evident from the widespread lay involvement in devotional activities, charitable fund-raising, in the moral and physical support provided to the clergy, and, above all, in rapidly expanding attendance at Catholic schools.

It was a powerfully effective culture that came to characterise English Catholicism as it reshaped itself. The secular priests were the real source of local initiatives and creative energy, and a different sort of priest was produced, with qualities and skills undreamt of in earlier generations. Priestly identity within the Catholic community was transformed, and a growing sense of corporate identity emerged, shaped by the traditions and lifestyle of expanding seminaries at home and abroad.

Copious provision was put in place for seminary formation, so that the priesthood was open, for the first time, to working class boys, and it became an option for a larger number of intelligent, pious, but poor Catholic boys in the cities of Victorian England and Wales. For the first time since the Reformation, Catholic priests in England had a strong sense of themselves as a distinct body of men, set aside for a particular service, with the training, authority and resources required to fulfil it. The priest as peripatetic missioner, with no fixed abode, was supplanted by the missionary rector with the right of settlement, and the duties and responsibilities of leadership within the local communities. As Catholicism expanded and became predominantly urban and working class, the priest had great freedom to become powerful and authoritarian. He established the community, raised the money, bought the land and built the church, and often the school, and this is how the story is often recounted in parish histories. The missionary rector was the creator of the buildings that gave the community a sense of identity and its place within English society.

In the midst of the great revival, there was, however, unease. One of its chief architects, William Bernard Ullathorne, Bishop of Birmingham was, in the 1880s, pessimistic about the missionary capacity of the Catholic Church in England. He observed that social factors, including the effects of industrial life in the cities, poor housing and the coarse company which Catholic youths encountered in factories, combined with mixed marriages, which all the bishops saw as a scourge, were wholly negative. Despite the huge emphasis that Ullathorne placed on seminary formation in his own diocese, he was not confident about the capacity of the clergy to embrace the future. 'The clergy are so fond of independence. Since my younger days the whole tone of things is utterly changed, and one is obliged to think a great deal about their feelings to save a great deal of difficulty'. [99]

The Eternal Priesthood

*Each of you has received a special grace, so, like good
stewards responsible for all these different graces of
God, put yourselves at the service of others.*

(I Peter 4: 10)

During the later nineteenth century, increasing attention was paid to the identity of the secular priesthood. Its formation and way of life became more distinctive, as it emerged into a new world of public ministry and leadership after the long period of Recusancy. The most famous and enduring discussion of these themes, published in 1883, was Cardinal Henry Edward Manning's *Eternal Priesthood*.[100] He had been developing his thoughts since the 1850s, as expressed in a private memo of that time:

> Far too few secular priests, especially in large towns; life of priest is therefore very laborious and able to do nothing but attend to the daily and hourly needs of people; habits of study become impossible, preparation for preaching neglected; any other work beyond the immediate, with communities or charities is neglected; life of priest becomes laborious and isolated, with little support or community life; need for a body of priests to continue studies and to undertake tasks that do not fall within power or range of existing parochial clergy; they should live together under a rule of life consistent with spirit of secular clergy; should be

exercised particularly in hearing confessions and spiritual guidance.[101]

Manning's concerns for the quality of priesthood, spiritual formation, greater pastoral and theological understanding, together with the need for study and reflection, and for fraternal support, all found their clearest expression in his foundation of the Oblates of St Charles, a sodality of secular priests sharing a common life, modelled on the reforms of St Charles Borromeo. His was also a strongly juridical model of priesthood, based on 'divine stewardship, the guardianship of the Blessed Sacrament and power to dispense the sacrament of the Eucharist'. That guardianship extended to the souls placed in his care, and the priest was teacher, guide and judge, a steward set over the household to guide and govern.

> Priests are fellow builders with God in edifying the Church, raising temples of the Holy Spirit and fathers of those whom they have baptised... The title of Father is the first, the chief, the highest, the most potent, the most persuasive, the most honourable of all the titles of a priest.[102]

Manning's *Eternal Priesthood* sought to put into practice many of the ideals of the Council of Trent, relating the English situation to Tridentine theology of priesthood and the work of a priest in a particular local context. Manning's vision was to elevate the standing of the secular priesthood and to inculcate a sense of priests being part of the professional classes. He sought to establish regularity and discipline of life and a measure of common life with other priests, and seminary was where preparation for this ideal life took place.[103] The highest possible standards were expected: 'Priests are also judges of men and physicians, and to perfect others requires perfection in himself'.[104]

Manning's vision of the priest as a member of the professional classes reflected the wider phenomenon of the professionalization of clergy in Victorian society. The rise of the specialist, separately educated clergyman, alongside the engineer, lawyer and physician, redefined the popular perception of all clergy. He became a respected public figure in Victorian society, but this exposed him to criticism and suspicion of his influence. This was particularly true of Catholic priests, now more numerous and visible at all social levels. By the late nineteenth century, priests were increasingly the butt of late Victorian prurience and hostility. A combination of enhanced status within the Catholic community, accompanied by increased suspicion from non-Catholics was the common experience of priests.

The Eternal Priesthood was largely the product of discussions with Ullathorne who was also preoccupied with the identity and wellbeing of the secular priesthood in the new environment. This was a concern that he frequently shared with John Henry Newman, as he dreamed of a separate, Tridentine seminary in Birmingham, free of the worldly culture of Oscott. He achieved this when he founded an entirely new seminary at Olton in 1873. Built on a shoestring and never completed, Olton was very different in spirit from Oscott. Ullathorne allowed neither staff nor students to transfer from Oscott to Olton.

When Newman preached at the opening of Olton, he warned the seminarians to prepare for a time of 'darkness different in kind from any that has been before it'. In his mind was the beginning of the rampant culture of atheism and hostility to religion. He saw that English Catholicism was emerging into a wider world, in which 'we shall be so large that our concerns cannot be hid, and at the same time so unprotected that we cannot but suffer'. The only protection, he insisted, was a strong body of priests who had a solid spiritual and theological formation in the seminary, and who were united in fraternity with their bishop and with each other.[105]

Herbert Vaughan, who succeeded Manning at Westminster, shared Newman's view. His approach is reflected in *The Young Priest*, a series of conferences collected and published posthumously in 1904, in which he laid great stress on the distinctiveness of clerical life, and the need for direction in the early years after ordination to prevent a loss of spiritual growth.[106] Vaughan's language emphasised servitude, self-sacrifice and the struggle to be worthy of the priestly calling. He spelt out three 'Causes of Failure' in a priest: the first was a want of 'that spirit of separation and unworldliness which hinders a priest from keeping his mind and heart far enough away from the world'; the second was 'the want of generous and disinterested zeal'; but the 'great wound' was the 'weakening of priestly spirit'. By this, Vaughan meant the danger inherent in a priest accommodating himself too much to the spirit of the world, and allowing himself to be influenced by the 'bitter enemy', the compromise with secular life.[107]

There is considerable evidence of concern about the capacity of men to live out the life of a priest, to sustain the necessary spiritual and physical energy, to resist the lure of the world's values, and to live up to their calling. This was not only a matter of concern for English bishops. Ullathorne's European contacts included Bishop Felix Dupanloup of Orleans, who, in the 1860s, sponsored the publication of a biography of Bartholomew Holzhauser. The seventeenth century Bavarian priest, whose Secular Clergy Institute had so appealed to the English Cardinal Philip Howard, had slipped into obscurity for over a century.

Dupanloup, in his introduction to Holzhauser's biography, identified afresh the problems associated with the 'indescribable solitariness, loneliness and cramped retirement' that priests could endure. He praised the idea of some sort of common life, 'where in the exercise of a bracing, brotherly love, they could free themselves from the cramping and weakening influences of their desolate lives of the past'.[108] He thought that Holzhauser provided this, and commended it to his English friend. Holzhauser became the inspiration for Ullathorne's new seminary at Olton.

The revival of interest in Holzhauser led to the formation of the Apostolic Union of Secular Priests, based on the Institute, which spread worldwide. It was approved by Pope Leo XIII and, in 1903, was taken under the patronage of Pius X, who was himself a member. Its purpose was to unite secular priests more closely in a fraternal bond of support, friendship and interdependence, bringing to the relatively isolated life of the secular priest an experience of common life. It had a rule of life inculcating regularity in prayer and examination of conscience, frequent meetings with a mentor, and, where possible, some sort of shared life.[109]

One of the small number of priests formed at the short-lived seminary at Olton was Henry Parkinson, who became rector of Oscott for twenty-eight years, where he instilled Holzhauser's vision into the life of the seminary. Parkinson founded the Birmingham diocesan branch of the Apostolic Union of Secular Priests in 1890, and Oscott was the only English seminary to have its own branch. He became the national organiser for England and Wales, and reports flowed in to him from diocesan branches, including Westminster, Hexham and Newcastle, Southwark, and from Scotland. Parkinson organised monthly retreats and maintained a regular correspondence with every member in the country. A requirement of membership was that each member submitted a monthly account of his fulfilment of the fixed *ratio* of prayers. The *ratio* gave Parkinson a simple mechanism for keeping in regular touch with members, and he continued this work until his death in 1924. The Apostolic Union outlived Parkinson, but membership gradually waned without his dogged commitment. By the 1940s, the rigidity of the *ratio* was widely regarded as too burdensome,[110] although the Birmingham branch continued to be listed in the Diocesan Directory until 1962.

The Apostolic Union was not the only instrument for the enhancement of clerical *esprit de corps*. One of the effects of larger, more structured and enclosed seminaries was a stronger sense of clerical identification with their *alma mater*. This was enhanced by the eradication of shared education, ensuring the development of networks of friendship exclusively within the priesthood, and a very clear sense of separate priestly identity.

By the 1890s there were nine seminaries in England and four overseas. The attempts to establish further seminaries failed, until St John's College, Wonersh opened in the early twentieth century. An attempt at consolidation of resources in the Central Seminary was established briefly at Oscott by Archbishop Edward Ilsley and Cardinal Herbert Vaughan in 1897. Francis Bourne, Vaughan's successor, was more determined than his predecessor had been about the importance of a diocesan seminary, where the bishop was able to keep close contact, and, as a result, he killed off the Central Seminary in 1907. There was no longer any national plan, as Vaughan had envisaged, but, under Bourne, the shape of seminaries took root that would last until the late 1960s. As a young priest, he was placed in charge of the new Southwark diocesan seminary at Wonersh. His attitudes and ideas had been shaped by his experience of formation in the Sulpician seminary in Paris. This was an 'uncompromisingly Tridentine' tradition of rigorous intellectual formation.[111]

Seminaries were increasingly staffed by priests with qualifications obtained abroad, mostly in Rome, and the teaching reflected European Neo-Scholasticism, but it was forced to adapt to English circumstances.[112] There was an emphasis on apologetics and on defending the Church against attack, which reflected the 'embattled' mindset of English Catholicism, with its powerful folk memory of persecution and continuing awareness of easily roused anti-Catholicism. The emphasis at Wonersh under Bourne, however, was on spiritual formation based on a Sulpician model, with only the most able being pushed intellectually, with a view to future staffing of the seminary. The atmosphere was familial rather than institutional, with 'a lightness of touch and informality' in dealings between staff and students.[113] By the early twentieth century, there was, nonetheless, a greater emphasis in English seminaries on formation for priesthood conducted in an atmosphere of simplicity of life and intellectual rigour.

At both Oxford and Cambridge, schemes were launched for a house of studies to enhance the theological education of secular priests. St Edmund's House, Cambridge struggled to find the resources and manpower to sustain itself, and St Charles' House, Oxford fizzled out. The failure of the Oxford house of studies revealed much about the conflicts over the formation of priests in the first decades of the twentieth century. Parkinson, as rector of Oscott, was lukewarm about the Oxford project, and the principal of St Charles' House rounded on him, insisting that 'those who want the diocese to be well staffed would welcome a new start' rather than the present 'deplorably low standard all round'. Moreover: 'It is not only low standards that are in the way, but, what is worse, self-complacency and complete illusion'.[114] O'Dowd wrote revealingly in his fury to Parkinson, about the 'foolhardy disagreements in policy that have been the bane of ecclesiastical education in England during the last twenty five years', which were now damaging his project. Parkinson's belief that only men safely ordained should be exposed to the possible dangers of a secular university was shared, and in 1918, the Holy See issued a decree forbidding attendance at lay universities by clerics not yet ordained, despite a petition from Archbishop Ilsley for exemption.[115]

Externally, English Catholicism expanded, and the number of men passing through seminaries increased, but this masked a narrowness, caution and restraint. William Godfrey, who was on the staff at Ushaw for twelve years and rector of the English College, Rome for eight years, finally succeeding Cardinal Hinsley at Westminster in the 1940s, embodied more than anyone the seminary spirit of the first half of the twentieth century. His book, *The Young Apostle*, published in 1924, summed up everything about his approach. The highly structured and disciplined spirituality that Godfrey inculcated in the seminary, with little place for the individual sense of vocation, dominates the book. It followed the ideas of Manning and Vaughan, but his attempt to transpose them for the twentieth century became increasingly unconvincing.

Many of Godfrey's contemporaries as rectors were disciplinarians, running highly structured seminaries, timetabled to inculcate an air of business and a capacity to switch from one activity to another adeptly. Rules and regulations were intended to form character and suppress human instinct. Seminary life was not easy, nor was it meant to be. As preparation for priesthood, detachment became characteristic of the way of life of the seminarian, not only from family but even from fellow clergy.

Godfrey's rigorous views, however, resonated in England, where they could be related to the sufferings of penal times. His own devotion to the English Reformation martyrs, many of them secular priests beatified in 1886, 1895 and 1929, suggested a connection between enduring hardship in seminary and the sufferings of the martyrs. It also recalled a time when the priest on the mission was a loner, caring not only for others, but his own salvation too, with scant support. Like his Recusant forebears, the twentieth century priest had to develop a self-made, do-it-yourself spirituality. For the vast majority, the life of a secular priest was one of independence and self-reliance. As numbers increased, this life was more likely to be lived out as part of an ordered presbyterium in a parish, where the parish priest exercised a high degree of authority, replicating that of the seminary.

When James Dey, who, after nearly thirty years as a military chaplain, became rector of Oscott, he tried to treat the students of the early 1930s as officers and gentlemen. One priest recalled, over fifty years later, his relief that he had been at Oscott in Dey's time, because, before then, there were seemingly endless rules. Dey had announced on his arrival that, 'There are no rules of this house – but some wishes of the community'.

> Mgr Dey was for introducing the way of mutual trust and free discipline which exists among a group of officers. He thought that the students should be regarded as officers in God's army and that they were mature enough, sincere enough and sufficiently educated to act as gentlemen, if they were treated as such.[116]

It became clear that most students were not ready for that level of responsibility. The experiment was something of a curate's egg, and was rapidly reversed by his successor.

Seminary training, as it developed in the twentieth century, cut priests off from worldly influences and from the intellectual life of universities and colleges, but also from the laity and, to some extent, from each other. The seminary was regarded as a more than adequate grounding in theology, providing all that was needed to fulfill the vision of priesthood, as something set apart, sacred and radically different from the laity. This cut off seminarians from their roots in the Catholic community, but also, deliberately, guarded them against acquiring the air of elitism associated, in many clerical minds, with universities and with Anglican clergy. In the seminaries, they were able to maintain a sense of distinctiveness and of authority, to imbibe a strong sense of clerical identity, but also, as became clearer in more recent years, to hide from real engagement with their own personal identity, to endure isolation and depression and to learn habits of bullying and manipulation.

Missionary Priest or Professional Cleric?

With heaven my throne and earth my footstool, what house could you build me?

(Isaiah 66: 1)

This approach to being a missionary priest was a long way from that of the Recusant period. Relationships between priest and laity had been transformed, not always for the better. Stress on priestly virtues of loyalty, certainty of answers, strict discipline and unquestioning obedience, meant that the priest was viewed as a 'man apart'. English Catholicism, until about 1950, embodied an emphasis on a transcendent God, a hierarchically structured church, and an authoritarian clergy properly distanced from the laity.[117] There was, at the same time, an instinct to professionalize the priesthood, and to make some provision for distinctive and clerical professional development.

One result of this was the founding of *The Clergy Review* in 1931, which, in its third incarnation as *The Pastoral Review*, continues publication. The editorial board, chaired by Archbishop Downey of Liverpool, consisted of the rectors of all the English seminaries, and the editors, Edward Myers, and Thomas Flynn, were both former rectors. Setting out the purpose of the journal in their first editorial, they declared, 'we are, in the first instance, seminary priests writing for seminary priests'. Its content was serious and scholarly, containing substantial essays and articles on topics of interest, as well as book reviews, Vatican documents, surveys of recent research, and, as in the modern *Pastoral Review*, notes for preachers.

The professional priest now had his *vade mecum*, which was in clear continuity with the rigidities and limitations of the seminary. The correspondence columns are revealing: concerned priests requesting guidance on topics such as the legality of school girls strewing flowers before the Blessed Sacrament in procession, on what ruling existed on the 'specific' prayers for the Holy Father in order to gain a plenary indulgence, and whether the rubric about lighting a third candle at the elevation during Mass was obligatory. Reassuringly, unless the bishop ruled otherwise, it was 'praiseworthy' but not obligatory. Priests and congregations were locked into a form of Catholic life that was dominated by regulation.

None of the standard works that reflect the understanding of priesthood in England from the 1860s to the 1960s, addressed the topic of priestly fraternity and common life, in the way that Holzhauser and the founders of the Apostolic Union had envisaged. The place of any intentional mutual support was neglected in Manning's *Eternal Priesthood*, in Bernard Ward's *The Priestly Vocation* (1918), in William Godfrey's *The Young Apostle* (1924) and in Ronald Knox's retreat conferences published in 1958 as *The Priestly Life*. It was taken for granted, perhaps, that the common identity of priesthood would be an automatic result of seminary formation, but the seminary emphasis on priestly detachment began to separate them from the world of the people they served, and, increasingly, from fellow priests.

The number of clergy and laity grew rapidly in the first half of the twentieth century, building on the great campaigns of the Victorians. Ordinations almost doubled in number between the wars from 119 in 1913 to 215 in 1939, yet anxiety about the shortage of priests persisted. Lay and clerical numbers peaked in the interwar years, and parishes multiplied in the hope of continued expansion in numbers, and numbers seemed to define what was important. During the 1940s, the total number of priests in England and Wales rose by 15% from 5,642 in 1939 to 6,643 in 1949.[118] The newly developed parish identity of Catholicism in England became a powerful focus for laity and clergy, and continued building and development was the task to which most priests gave their energy.

The massive building programme exacerbated the effects of the rigid seminary model that inculcated a sense of individual authority and separation from the laity, from wider society and, often from each other. Building a new church or school became widely regarded as a mark of achievement in the life of a parish priest. This enabled and even encouraged the priest to create separate 'clerical' spaces in the sacristy and presbytery. The overall effect could be to isolate priests, and to encourage an unhealthy mentality of solitary independence, and an identity associated with buildings. The clericalisation of religious space and the sense of ownership of the parish and its fabric that took root was in stark contrast to the recusant mission of earlier centuries. Much of the capacity for flexibility and responsiveness and the sharing of resources with laity was lost. The priest became the metaphorical king in his castle, dispensing authority and sacramental grace according to a legalistic framework. Clerical identity replaced priestly identity.

One guide, *Practical Suggestions for the Newly Ordained*,[119] published in 1930 with Cardinal Bourne's support, and no doubt typical of its time, set out where the newly ordained priest stood in relation to the presbytery and the parish priest, and, therefore, what his model of presbytery life was to be. It made clear that, while the presbytery was the curate's home, it was the parish priest who was responsible for its arrangements. The good curate would not be noisy around the house and would be considerate of 'the domestics' and the other resident priests in the care of common spaces. Mealtimes must be observed and smoking after lunch should follow the lead of whoever sat at the head of the table. Much of this, quaint though it now seems, reflected the *mores* of middle class life in the inter-war years, but the emphasis for the curate was on 'conforming himself to his present customs and surroundings'.[120]

The tone of the *Practical Suggestions* was one of hard work, conformity and restraint. It largely consisted of exactly what it set out in the title: practical tips on performing the pastoral and liturgical tasks to be undertaken. Hobbies were encouraged, holidays somewhat grudgingly recommended, with the permission of the parish priest and the vicar general, but nowhere is there any mention of the value of human friendship. The last chapter, perhaps predictably, was entitled 'Some Warnings'. The dangers warned against are also predictable, but revealing of their time: sloth or idleness, excessive use of alcohol, and the unnamed danger, coyly hedged around with admonitions about avoiding 'a fall' or 'a mistake', from which the newly ordained priest was supposed to draw conclusions about the risk of sexual relationships.[121]

Idleness was still regarded as a grave danger in the 1950s, which, in Ronald Knox's view, had become associated with a sense of drudgery, boredom and routine with the passage of years in ministry, leaving priests open to the loss of zeal and energy, leading to the sin of 'accidie'.[122] There was still no mention of the value of priestly fraternal support or mentoring by another, more experienced priest; the solution, if there was one, had to be found from within.

> Tell Almighty God that he has, for whatever reason, made you, at least for the time being, a hewer of wood and a drawer of water in his service; it seems for the moment all you can aspire to; very well, you will perform this humble office, faithfully, to prove your love for him....Make up as best you can, by your humility, and by a kind of dogged obedience, for all the priestly qualities he sees lacking in you.[123]

The aspect of parochial ministry given most attention in Dunford's 1930 guide, and others, was household visiting, which was regarded as having unique value, and therefore was expected to take up a considerable amount of the time and energy of assistant priests. It was anticipated that priests would visit households, partly to cajole or admonish the lax attenders at Mass and the sacraments, and partly in an effort to know the people whom the priest was sent to serve. Dunford dismisses briskly any misguided notion that there is not much use in visiting the people: 'results prove the falseness of this'.[124]

Writing in 1966, Cardinal John Carmel Heenan, himself ordained in 1930, continued to emphasise this uniquely English practice of household visiting, unknown in other European Churches. He insisted that, despite changing social customs, education and living conditions, 'visiting the homes of our people is the most rewarding of all our pastoral work. Dull and laborious, it is nevertheless the most reliable test of priestly zeal'.[125] He seemed uncertain about whether it was the people or the priest who benefitted from visiting, and whether it inspired the priest, or was a 'dull' act of duty. He did recognise, however, the limitations of his own generation, when priests were more 'reserved' with each other. 'The parish priest was recognised as *primus inter pares*, but there was more often emphasis on the *primus* than the *pares*. The parish priests of yesterday were children of their day'.[126]

Looking back over fifty years of priesthood, James Crichton was more sceptical, recalling visiting, in his early days in the 1930s, as 'an obsession'.

> Urban parishes in those days were very densely populated, and if one succumbed to the pressure to visit as many houses as possible one learned after a few years' experience that spiritually speaking it was unproductive...You could exhort people to go to Mass if they were not going (as frequently was the case) but your words conveyed next to nothing of spiritual value.[127]

He recognised, however, the importance of a priestly presence, and reflected that visitation could take on a different quality. If it had a focus on real and sustained help and support to fewer people, rather than the obsessive fulfilment of a routine duty, it sometimes resulted in a real conversion of heart. Crichton cites the not infrequent example in the cities of the 1930s, of supporting families where tearaway sons had been brought to court for petty crime.

In 1950, the centenary of the Restoration of the Hierarchy was celebrated. In Archbishop George Beck's volume of commemorative essays, his extraordinary conclusion was that,

> Signs are not wanting, however, that the drift to materialism is at an end...The day of doctrine is returning and for that reason alone, the situation provides an opportunity and a challenge to the Church in this country.[128]

He was explicit that the task of the Church was to 'teach the faith of Christ and administer the sacraments'. The history of a century of expansion was a cause for the sort of self-congratulation expressed by Beck, and of a rather simplistic view of the challenges facing English Catholicism. He missed many of the signs of the times.

From Across the Sea: the Irish Dimension

*My dwelling is plucked up and removed from me
like a shepherd's tent.*
(Isaiah 38: 12)

The single most significant influence on English Catholicism in the period between roughly 1850 and 1960 was Irish migration, not only within the Catholic population in general, but within the secular priesthood. By 1850, it had become obvious to the new English Catholic hierarchy that its existing cohort of priests could not cope with the massive influx of impoverished, poorly educated Irish migrants, leaving a rural peasant life for the crush of Victorian industry. The Irish priest became a necessity in preserving the faith of the migrant population, and the particularity of the relationship between priest and people in Ireland shaped the next fifty years.

There is no doubt that in rural Ireland Catholic priests were invested with an authority which combined cultural *mores* and spirituality. Priests were said to have an almost mystical hold over their flock....Although the average Irish Catholic did not believe that priests had magical powers, the sense of respect that surrounded the priest – especially the Irish priest – was palpable.[129]

Active recruitment of seminarians and priests in Ireland was organized by English dioceses, struggling to cope with newly expanded, mainly culturally Irish, parishes. From the early twentieth century Irish migration began to decline, and the 'Irish Catholic' was more likely to be the child or grandchild of migrants. Social and economic mobility became more fluid, with emergent Irish middle and professional classes in most cities. 'By the inter-war years...Catholicism not Irishness provided the key cultural marker for a majority of Irish in Britain.'[130]

In the 1920s and 1930s, priests were regularly incardinated directly from Irish dioceses into the Archdiocese of Birmingham. In the diocese of Salford in the late nineteenth century, 38% of clergy were Irish born, and by the 1920s, this had increased to 46%.[131] One of them was Henry Vincent Marshall, who became bishop of the diocese from 1939 to 1955, and had a reputation for turning down applicants for the priesthood who were not of Irish extraction. He was not alone in this policy. A recent study of the Diocese of Middlesbrough has revealed the extent to which its presbyterate was dominated by Irish recruitment for much of the twentieth century.[132]

By 1950, urban Catholic population was growing rapidly, due to the social and economic effects of industrial and commercial expansion. After World War II, Irish migration to Britain hit peaks unknown since the 1850s, promoted by Irish economic stagnation and the post-war reconstruction of Britain. Between 1951 and 1961, more than 400,000 people crossed the Irish Sea, two-thirds of them finding their way to London.[133] Many of them made their new lives in nursing in the newly founded National Health Service, or in the building trades. As well as leaving a stagnant economy, Irish migrants were leaving a country where the Church represented 'the ultimate authority'.[134]

In places, this authority became authoritarianism, with devastating human and social results. Many of those who left were women seeking greater marital freedom and opportunity, and teenagers looking for a different future.

> While many were dedicated and regular churchgoers, finding the Church both spiritually and socially rewarding, others left Ireland to get away from the dominating priests and stifling Catholic dogma for independent careers and life of their own, or perhaps in search of a husband or wife.[135]

There was fear among priests in Ireland that migrants would lose their faith in Britain, which perhaps encouraged a large number of priests to follow the laity across the sea. Ironically, whether or not the laity left to escape the Church, once out of Ireland, migrants clung to it as a source of social, spiritual and even economic support. In reality, it was the Church in Britain that would end up being stretched in providing many of the networks of support inevitably needed, and some priests were openly critical of Irish parents who encouraged their children to leave home.[136]

By 1961, 30% of secular clergy in England and Wales were Irish-born, but a far higher proportion came from Irish migrant families resident in England. They brought a different tradition to bear on priestly identity, including a strong political dimension that could sit uncomfortably in English society, and a rigorism inherent in Irish seminaries. They also brought a strong tradition of clerical authority and lay obedience to bear.

There is a received idea that Irish priests were imbued with Jansenist ideology, imported into Ireland by the priests trained in France during penal times. This notion seems to have little to support it. The Irish Catholic tradition was certainly rigorous, from its Augustinian monastic origins, but while there may have been Irish Jansenists in the modern period, there was no Irish Jansenism. The Irish resistance to authority was not that of continental Jansenism opposed to papal interference, but of a Catholic people who had endured centuries of Protestant imperialism.

> Popular rigorism derived from tradition and monastic heritage—the remote past—was quite different from the "university, elitist" reform movement (1615-1789) of the Early Modern period on the European Continent.... whatever Jansenism was, it was not Irish. Some say, without proof, that "Jansenistic priests" took refuge in Ireland and spread their ideas to the people. But this hearsay remains hearsay....The Irish clergy who were educated abroad may have been aware of Continental controversies, but importing these battles would have bewildered the average Irish Catholic.[137]

Nevertheless, the effects of this tradition of rigour and resistance on the nature of English Catholic life, and on the culture of priesthood were immense. The clergy were 'in an unrivalled position to influence how adherents lived their lives and practiced their faith...as a rule, priests preferred the laity to passively obey their will'.[138]

This was achieved, as far as possible, by a renewed emphasis on home visiting, to encourage, cajole or persuade Catholics to greater devotional and religious practice, especially Mass attendance. Priests also became well-known public figures in predominantly Irish areas of cities, exercising a social role as keepers of order and good behaviour among children. It is suggested that 'anxiety about priestly retribution' was weaker among the second or third generation Irish, than among the newly arrived Irish born, perhaps reflecting their recent recollection of the greater power wielded by priests in Ireland.[139] If this was the case, the gradual generational change in the composition of the Irish Catholic population may well explain the waning of clerical power as succeeding generations became more Anglicised.

By 1971, a quarter of Catholics in Britain were Irish immigrants, but a further 20% were second generation Irish.[140] The passing of the single generation of post-war Irish migrants was under way, and was beginning the reshaping of the composition of Catholic parishes. The close knit working class urban communities of Irish began to disappear, as social and economic mobility enabled the drift to the suburbs, or slum dwellers were resettled in anonymous housing estates.

There clearly was a generational change under way, as Desmond Ryan noted in his study based on interviews two decades later. 'A number of priests commented on the lack of rancour with which the Irish-background young people gave up practice, and the absence of any attempt to rationalize it. They just stopped coming'.[141] The generational shift also had a huge effect on the priesthood. It has been shown, in an unpublished study based on the Archdiocese of Birmingham, traditionally a strongly Irish diocese, that by the 1990s, half of the priests aged 60-79 identified themselves as Irish, whilst a third of those between 40-59, and only a quarter of those under forty did so, as the effects of post-war migration waned.[142]

Social and economic transformation in the late 1950s, when Prime Minister Harold Macmillan told Britain that 'it had never had it so good', was also affecting Catholic life. Cities, where the majority of Catholics were to be found, were transformed in post-war redevelopment schemes, often, it seemed, designed to imitate the increasingly familiar images of

American life on TV screens and in films. At the beginning of the 1960s, studies of Catholic parishes and social change were already revealing that traditional parish structures, 'might not be adequate to meet the needs of and multiple problems of a modern urban civilization' and that the structure had 'not as yet adapted itself sufficiently to the new conditions and to a changed situation in the mid twentieth century.'[143] The conversion of England to Catholicism had begun to look less likely. Yet, for long afterwards, the Catholic community continued building, confident that there would be laity and clergy to occupy the spaces.

What are Priests for?

Rejoice in your hope, be patient in tribulation,
be constant in prayer.
(Romans 12: 12)

The laity was, at the same time, increasingly finding its own education and formation in morality and doctrine, thus developing its own opinions. The hugely successful school building programme, ensuring Catholic primary and secondary schools across the country, with government support, was bearing fruit in academic achievement. The implementation of the 1963 Robbins Report, which doubled university intake between the late 1960s and early 1970s, alongside the rise of polytechnics and the founding of the Open University in 1969, opened the doors. Thousands of Catholics, alongside many others, were the first generation of their families to enter the expanding world of higher education.

The bishops had encouraged lay associations and popes addressed encyclicals over the heads of clergy, so 'they could hardly object when the laity took to debate and the correspondence columns of the newspapers'.[144] What was new was that competence in decision making was becoming no longer just the preserve of the clergy. Educationally, the laity were as well, if not better, equipped to assess questions, and were eager to do so. Lay and clerical Catholics entering the newly expanding world of higher education took up, not only theology, but the new academic disciplines, including sociology, and began to apply them to the Catholic world around them, investigating and commenting upon the phenomenon identified as 'secularisation'.

One of them at least, suggested that secularisation was a lazy generalisation for what was really happening to the clergy: shortage of priests, decline in the social status of ministry, and uncertainty about the role of the priest.[145] That uncertainty was not brought about by the Second Vatican Council, as some commentators superficially asserted, but was closely related to changes in society that questioned the role of clergy in general. Affluent societies, by the 1960s, were increasingly defining people, especially men, by what they did, by their occupation: so what did a priest 'do'? As Towler suggested, it would have been meaningless to ask medieval priests what they 'did'.

> They fulfilled a most important function in society, but it was a function not restricted to ministry within the Church. It extended to the effective ministry of society as a whole, and comprised many occupations and various callings.[146]

The context in which the priest's role had meaning, by the 1960s, was defined in terms of his relationship to members of the Church. Apart from the sacramental functions attached to ordination, there was a tide of opinion in Catholicism that interpreted the Council's teachings as a mandate to give more 'functions' to lay people, and, therefore, to question what priests were for. As priests and laity began to be seen more in terms of function or occupation than relationship, uncertainty about priestly role and identity became more prevalent.

This contributed to what has been described as a paradigmatic shift from a mechanistic to a more organic model of the Church. It led to conflicts between the two models, and a crisis of authority between those clergy and laity who viewed authority as an intrinsic value, and those who viewed it as a means to an end.[147] Until the 1950s, the broadly mechanistic model seemed to work in England, within an apparently unchanging and stable church. The hierarchical model was 'explicit and pervasive'. The priest was seen as a sacred person, whose inherent dignity separated him from the laity, over whom he was superior. The laity were socialised to a proper deference to clergy, whose authority was rarely questioned.[148]

The paradigmatic shift, however, occurred not only in the Church. Catholics, including those who entered seminaries and were ordained, were the children of a changing society, in which deference was fast disappearing. The enclosed Catholic subculture of late Victorian England was no longer, if it ever had been, impenetrable. Catholics were just as much a part of the 'rock and roll' generation of the 1950s and the flower power hippydom of the 1960s as their contemporaries. This generation of young Catholics were equipped to inform themselves and to make their own moral and political choices, based not only on what they heard from the pulpit or read in the Catholic press, but what they absorbed from television, radio and from their non-Catholic friends. A chaplain at Liverpool University in the 1960s, Fr McGoldrick, commented presciently:

> There is not much anti-clericalism in this country, even among intellectuals, but a great lack of understanding could grow up because priests and educated laity are not speaking the same language.[149]

This was the context within which the Second Vatican Council was received in England and Wales. An educated and articulate laity could buy copies of the Council documents in paperback at their High Street bookshop, as they picked up the latest Edna O'Brien or David Lodge novel of Catholic angst. The laity did not have to wait to be told what to think by the parish priest or bishop. The clergy could no longer command a united front themselves in light of *Humanae Vitae,* together with changing approaches to theology after the Second Vatican Council. The assumptions that Manning, Vaughan and Godfrey had made about seminaries were no longer watertight, and questions were being asked about whether seminaries were the best way of training priests.

The institutional and numerical crises of English Catholicism in the latter half of the twentieth century are well charted. Less fully explored is what happened to those 'missionary priests' who had become entrepreneurs and professional specialists in pastoral leadership of a particular kind, when tight Catholic parish identities started to disperse. The Church within and beyond England and Wales was asking itself questions about priesthood and the effectiveness of vocational discernment and seminary formation, long before the Second Vatican Council.

A report drawn up in England and Wales for a European conference on priestly vocations in 1958 is revealing. It described, historically, a change in the social status of secular priests from around 1860. The sons of the gentry, it was suggested, were more inclined to attend schools run by the Jesuits and Benedictines, who were more likely, therefore, to benefit from any vocations. Secular clergy vocations came mainly from 'good Catholic lower class families', and a smaller number from the business and professional classes. The rise of grammar schools, the report suggested, meant that academically bright boys who might previously have gone to seminary now remained at school until sixteen or eighteen, 'and it is a question, difficult to answer, whether a number of such boys do not lose their vocation in such surroundings'. Nevertheless, it was acknowledged that the new Catholic grammar schools could also be a fruitful source of vocations, and the majority of boys entering seminary from grammar school appeared to persevere to ordination.[150]

The report asserted that, at the end of the 1950s, the picture for the secular priesthood was 'far from bright'. The large increase in the number of priests, as a result of Irish recruitment, had masked the fact that the number of ordinations in England and Wales had dropped from 153 in 1937 to 147 in 1956, and the future prospect was not good. In 1958, there were a total of 869 seminarians, suggesting an average number of ordinations per year of 145. In England, there was one priest for every 809 Catholics, and this was possibly based on an underestimate of population. The warning was stark: 'more priests are needed'. Of the 3,590 secular priests at the time of the report, many were from Ireland, and the question was asked for how long the supply would continue. England, the report compilers bluntly stated, should provide her own priests; more native priests were needed 'and needed quickly'.[151]

The problems were not only to be found in England and Wales. The centenary of the death of the Curé d'Ars, in June 1959, was taken as an opportunity by the Congregation for Seminaries to address 'certain problems of ecclesiastical formation'. The language was uncompromising:

> The Sacred Congregation of Seminaries is convinced that, in this matter (personal holiness and interior life) much is left to be done in institutes for clerical training. In view of the attitude of young priests, particularly towards the problems of the ministry, the question arises whether the traditional principles of formation are not being overlooked.[152]

Six months later, the Congregation was urging local churches throughout the world to focus energy and manpower on fostering vocations.[153] Pope Pius XII had established a pontifical society for priestly vocations in 1941,[154] but progress was slow, and the first international congress of national vocations directors did not take place until 1966. No-one had been appointed to that role in England and Wales, suggesting that the promotion of priestly vocations was perhaps not being taken very seriously. Mgr Leo Alston, the rector of the English College, Rome, attended on behalf of England and Wales.[155]

A study of English Catholics by a non-Catholic journalist in 1967, complained that it was not easy to find out what went on in seminaries. The author remarked, of his first visit to Ushaw, on the sense of distance between priests at Ushaw and the non-Catholic visitor. 'It was not a question of active antagonism, but I was conscious of wandering in an alien atmosphere'.[156] He reported that a 1964 correspondence in the *Catholic Herald*, including critical letters written by seminarians, had stopped abruptly. It was said that such letters were the first ever published.[157] Not surprisingly, this provoked journalistic curiosity.

In general, reported the author, critics say that seminaries are out of date, in what they teach, in the attitudes they instil and their isolation from the rest of the community. The philosophical system was criticised for having no validity outside the Church, and decreasing acceptance by the better minds inside the Church.[158] No twentieth century philosophy was taught, and most of the theology was only taught to sustain dogmatic positions, not to test conclusions. Teaching methods dominated by the regurgitation of text books left many priests ill-equipped intellectually to address abstract ideas thrust at them in parish settings. There was little training in preaching or confessional practice, in the use of modern media, or in awareness of trade unions and politics, social issues or of other Christian denominations.

The impression gained was that priests were being trained to be leaders by being passive and unquestioning in obedience, thereby dulling their capacity for initiative and decision making. A host of petty restrictions inhibited personal responsibility and self-respect, meaning that obedience and submission to authority were qualities inseparable from priesthood. The most urgent and anxious criticisms focussed on physical isolation and educational segregation. Critics advocated the abolition of junior seminaries, and the introduction of practical, pastoral experience into seminary programmes, together with degree level theological studies.[159]

Immediately after the Council, Cardinal John Carmel Heenan published his own reflections on the decree *Presbyterium Ordinis* and its importance for priests in England and Wales.[160] While he harked back to the Church of his youth, and the 'fine old priests of earlier generations',[161] he recognised some of the current issues. *Presbyterium Ordinis* built on what Heenan interpreted as 'an evolving comradeship between priests' that made many of the older pastoral manuals, as illustrated above, seem so out of date. He acknowledged that 'the priest working in self-imposed isolation damages the mission of the Church'.[162]

Like most leaders of his generation, he floundered in the face of declining vocations and the rapidly advancing shortage of priests, blaming increased prosperity and changes in education, combined with what he called the disunity of the Church in the wake of the Council. He offered no solutions, other than to fall back on the traditional one, which was clearly failing. 'We must give our boys a vision. Parents and priests alone can do this....Holy priests make holy families. Holy families produce priests'.[163]

A 1970 account of contentious but inconclusive discussions about the future of junior seminaries in the north of England echoed what the 1959 Congregation for Seminaries document had hinted at. Junior seminaries were failing to provide the number of men needed to fill the senior seminaries, and 'late vocations', i.e. those men who had not been to junior seminaries, seemed to be proving more fruitful. By 1970, the language of crisis was being used about the recruitment of priests, with a growing recognition of at least some of the causes:

> The Church can expect to recruit suitable candidates only insofar as the life of the priest is worthwhile and is seen to be worthwhile. The present crisis in vocations to the priesthood can be largely attributed to the inadequate 'image' of the priesthood presented to young people today....What alienates young people more than anything is the fact that a priest is expected to do violence to his personality in order to fit in with *mores* which, so young people feel, are no longer a suitable expression of Christian generosity and service....He waits till over forty before being given initiative and responsibility, subject to excessive authority, jack of all trades, often out of date on key issues.[164]

Reforms in seminary formation and culture were believed to be the key to the change needed, and frequent discussions took place between the English seminaries throughout the 1970s about 'seminary lifestyles'. Priestly distinctiveness had become separation, with priests seeming too detached from the world of the people they served.

A Hunger for Priesthood

*Will you not restore again my life, that your
people may rejoice in you?*
(Psalm 84: 7)

Some responses to the loss of direction and to a reading of Conciliar reforms left the Church more clerical than before, as parishes abandoned 'old fashioned' lay orientated devotions, such as rosary and processions, and placed increasing emphasis on participation in the Mass. The priest traditionally used attendance at Mass as the vital benchmark of loyalty, and in modern church buildings counting could be done easily and accurately, and used as a regular measure. The counting began to reveal the uncomfortable reality that the laity were becoming less inclined to conform. Declining lay interest in the importance of attending Mass regularly cut at the very heart of Catholic identity; no longer the benchmark, it was becoming a matter of choice.

> The concept of the parish in urban communities has diminishing significance and diminishing relevance. The idea of community has faded, and image of parish was becoming more like a spiritual service station.[165]

The laity who remained became reoriented away from sacramental confession as the main source of reconciliation, to Holy Communion, so that attendance at Mass became even more obviously the single measure of Catholic identity and 'membership'. The 'full active and conscious participation' in the liturgy, advocated by *Sacrosanctum Concilium*, was taken to mean increased emphasis on the regular reception of Holy Communion, leading to an expectation that the priest was there to celebrate Mass, and not much else.[166]

Some priests wondered whether there were better, or at least different ways of living priestly life in a parish context. One of these was Michael Hollings, whose parish ministry in Southall, West London, as well as his time as chaplain at Oxford University, and in broadcasting, won him both plaudits and criticism, in equal measure. In his semi-autobiographical *Living Priesthood*,[167] published in 1977, Hollings identified issues that seemed shocking at the time, but have now become unresolved commonplaces, including the 'global Christian credibility gap between the "dying" north and west and the "starving" south and east', describing the developed world as like 'an aged alcoholic or drug addict' clutching greedily at the world's resources.[168]

He was critical of the insularity of parish life in his own western, English experience, becoming aware that the real hunger was not in the poorer parts of the world, but in the Christian heartland of Europe. 'Among many there is a loss of hope, growing inward looking materialism, and even despair, especially in the west'.[169] Hollings' solutions were radical, and therefore unlikely to find widespread and ready support, but he did not hold back in the ferocity of his language:

> We are at five minutes to midnight. We must open our eyes to the situation...as it is now. In order to see properly we need a spiritual revolution, emptying ourselves so that we may have in us the mind which is in Christ Jesus.... It is people, not property, organisations or buildings, the Church is in the world to present to Christ....We have allowed ourselves as a Church to be led up the cul-de-sac of worldly possessions and rising standards of living, so that our aims in education and preaching are basically more worldly, selfish and materialistic, than Christian.[170]

Catholics began to carry what Robin Gill called the 'millstones' that weigh down the churches and block vision. Gill suggested that, until the

1990s, the Catholic Church had bucked the trend of declining attendance experienced in other denominations. It did not suffer the depressive effects on the community of worshipping in half empty churches.[171] That was, in reality, no longer true even in the 1970s, although the Catholic community continued complacently to believe that it was.

Maintaining the commitment to buildings and meeting expectations of sacramental availability, with already dwindling numbers, trapped priests. They were left, at worst, with the unsatisfactory and impossible combination of janitor, universal social worker, and sacramental machine. Priestly identity was difficult to maintain, and even hard to discuss. It created a determination among some priests to break out of what had become more a 'clerical' identity than a priestly identity.

Dissatisfaction and disillusion, resulting from a degree of confusion over the priestly role, led to large scale abandonment by priests of public ministry, while increasingly well-educated sections of the laity became more confident and assertive. It was observed, in the mid 1980s, that older and 'higher class' people were more likely to report meaningful contact and personal interaction with a priest, and a strong sense of parish communal identity, while ties with younger, working class people were being lost. The closeness and personal contact between priests and laity changed from an emphasis on support and concrete help for struggling families, as reported by Crichton in the 1930s, to an exchange of cultural and religious dialogue between intellectual and social equals.[172]

In 1990, *The Tablet* commented on a mood of impatience at a meeting of bishops at Chur, Switzerland, at the perceived lack of progress since the Council. The Chur meeting was a prelude to the Synod of Bishops later that year, on the theme of priesthood. *The Tablet* also reported on the consultation in England and Wales in preparation for the Synod. The beatification in 1987 of eighty-five lay and ordained English martyrs, had perhaps reminded English Catholics of their inheritance, as the response to the Synod consultative process strongly emphasized that seminarians and priests should remember that England and Wales were missionary territory.[173] The missionary priest, the heir of the martyrs, was in need of a fresh vision, but few Catholics of a newly ecumenical generation, anxious to leave behind the 'ghetto' mindset associated with the Reformation and its aftermath, were willing to look to the inspiration of the past to find it.[174]

The 1990 synod resulted in the 1992 Apostolic Exhortation, *Pastores Dabo Vobis,* which, for the past twenty-five years, has been the guiding instrument in consideration of priesthood and priestly formation. By the end of the twentieth century, it was clear that the social, political and religious context in which Catholicism existed in England and Wales had been transformed. Extremes of affluence and poverty were commonplace, Britain's industrial heritage had all but disappeared and racially or religiously inspired violence was seen on the streets of Britain. The technological revolution in the ways in which the world not only works, but socializes, and even thinks, was already under way, offering undreamt of possibilities but also posing new problems.

This social transformation was accompanied by a curious, and dramatic, statistical phenomenon in English Catholicism. Between 1965 and 1996, Mass attendance dropped from 1.9 million to 1.1 million, the number of infant baptisms from 134,055 to 74,848, adult receptions from 14,803 to 6,133, marriages from 46,480 to 17,294, and the number of priests had slumped from 7,808 to 5,732. Yet, extraordinarily, the number of parishes had increased from 2,320 to 2,856.[175] The building instinct had still not lost its power, and these figures suggest a lack of strategic planning to meet population shifts created by fresh migration and urban regeneration schemes. New parishes were needed in areas of housing development on the outskirts of cities, but how much consideration was given to the resources needed to maintain all the existing commitments alongside the new ones, and whether it was desirable or achievable?

The sociologist, Michael Hornsby Smith suggested that there was a clear case for 'a rethinking of the pastoral priorities of a declining number of priests and the greater involvement of the laity in a wide range of pastoral ministries'. This appeared to have cautious episcopal support in the 1995 Working Party Report, *The Sign We Give,*[176] and in the 1997 *Ad Limina* Report:

> Pastors have a duty to foster the charisms, ministries and different forms of participation by the people of God, without adopting notions borrowed from democracy and sociology which do not reflect the Catholic vision of the Church and the authentic spirit of Vatican II.[177]

The Sign We Give developed the concept of 'collaborative ministry', while acknowledging that it was a cumbersome and somewhat unsatisfactory term.[178] The role of the priest, it proposed, was to 'effectively invite people to make full use of their gifts and energies in ministries and other activities (and)...let go of responsibilities and trust others with charge of various aspects of parish life and mission'.[179] This vision had a limited life, although aspects of it took shape in some parishes, but widespread enthusiasm and commitment were not forthcoming.

This perhaps reflected what Hornsby Smith has described as complacent, unchallenging and domesticated Catholicism, but also the increasing loss of confidence within the priesthood. The language of 'collaborative ministry' and 'lay ministries' seemed, to some priests, threatening rather than exciting. It was also true, in many situations, that where lay people were prepared to be drawn further into the mission, it was often in the areas of liturgy, pastoral planning and leadership, potentially undermining priestly identity just as much as the wealthy gentry or factory-owning patrons had done in the past.

The fundamental problem with all of this was that it perpetuated the functional idea of both priest and lay Catholic, concentrating on what individuals could or should do. This led to frustrated laity and disempowered priests, subject to equal measures of criticism for doing too much or too little. This 'functional' mood, coincided with the 'reconceptualization of the Eucharist – moving from its understanding as a sacrifice of the high priest on Calvary to the communal action of the people of God gathered to represent the sacred meal in the upper room'. This combination created greater scope for questions about, not only what the priest was for, but who the priest was. Serious debates and pressure groups began to form, to press for the ordination of married men, and of women.[180]

The last decade of the twentieth century saw a resurgence in published reflection on priesthood in this country, perhaps stimulated by the Synod and its resulting Apostolic Exhortation, along with the publication of *The Sign We Give*. Wisdom was needed in the light of the growing sense of crisis in the priesthood, by then exacerbated by the first waves of shocking cases of clerical child abuse. The radical transformation in attitudes to authority in the last decades of the twentieth century inevitably affected clerical authority within the Catholic community, but the waning of the culture of deference was nothing as compared to what hit Catholic society in the 1990s.

The trust and respect accorded to the priesthood both within the Church and beyond, was being rocked to its foundations, as more highly publicised evidence of serial sexual abuse emerged. This took place in a particular historical context in England and Wales. The tradition of trust and affection between Catholic laity and priests was strong and enduring, but the abuse scandals undermined it to an unprecedented extent. Non-Catholic prejudice and suspicion about the trustworthiness of Catholic priests was also deeply rooted; the popular perception of priests as duplicitous and dishonest stretches back to the sixteenth century.[181] Suspicion about Catholic priests could now appear, in the public mind, to be justified.

The effect of this on the morale of the majority of priests who remained engaged on the pastoral mission has been given little systematic attention. One controversial study, based on a survey of English priests carried out in 1996[182] reported that, on average, 68% of priests, across all age ranges, whether secular or regular, felt demoralised by the abuse scandals.[183] There is no reason to suppose that the proportion would have declined in the twenty years since that snapshot was taken, and a study based on interview data from the Archdiocese of Liverpool in 2008-9, echoed it.

> ...child abuse and the responses to it were the subject of a number of concerns alongside regret and compassion for the victims: that the fact of the abuse of children by priests (and the way it had been reported in some media) had seriously damaged the Church's mission and the reputation of the priesthood...that priests felt vulnerable to false allegations and that some had suffered from allegations being badly handled by the authorities.[184]

All priests and seminarians, over the last thirty years, have been affected by the criminal processes and the public response to them, and are tainted by association with forms of criminality that undermine everything about priesthood. It has the power, just as in the sixteenth century, to create a 'collective, if partly unconscious, self-perception of criminality'.[185] There is still a need to acknowledge the impact of this issue on morale and on the identity of priesthood. Trust between fellow priests, and between priests, bishops and laity, has been undermined to such an extent that it still cannot be fully aired. The unspoken conversation about response, loss of trust and morale still remains a block to the wellbeing of priests.

Michael Richards, theologian and sometime editor of the *Clergy Review*, Tony Philpot, an experienced seminary spiritual director and international *Responsabile* of the priestly Confraternity of Jesus Caritas, and Donal O'Leary, theologian and episcopal vicar for clergy in the Diocese of Leeds, were among those secular priests who grappled with at least some of the issues around priestly life and identity in the 1990s.

Richards addressed the question of the 'essence' of priesthood, articulated but not defined by the Second Vatican Council, which, in his view, had raised more questions than answers. He suggested that when priests, bishops and deacons found their true place in the priestly body of Christ, their confidence and energy would be restored.[186] How that was to be achieved was the problem. Richards was convinced that 'recovery will come in the first place, not by an attempt to restore the ritual-based image of the ordained ministry, but through a renewed conviction of the significance of the person of Jesus Christ in history, and consequently of the representatives he has chosen and sent out to do his work'.[187] Renewal would only come about if 'bishops, priests and deacons strengthen their understanding of themselves as people sent by God to build up believing communities'.[188] The challenge still remains of how that strengthened understanding can be brought about.

O'Leary wrote from a more obviously spiritual, mystical perspective, but in blunt language, about the 'strange malaise and doubt that springs from a newly-felt loneliness and from a lack of self-esteem and self-identity in our lives as priests during this critical transition time for the Church'.[189] He was outspoken in his assertions about the fearfulness and hopelessness he heard expressed by priests when challenged to 'call people into their true selves, to fulfil their own graced potential for beauty, to live more fully their own humanity'.[190] Just like Richards, O'Leary proposed that the self-evident starting point for renewal was the person of Jesus, but in dialogue with the wider world and with creation, a theme taken up afresh by Pope Francis in his 2015 encyclical *Laudato Sì*. O'Leary was ambitious in the models of priesthood he offered, and in the urgency and the need for renewal so much that his conclusion is monumental, but not altogether surprising:

To be a priest today takes all the life we have left to live. To be a priest today takes the heart of a hermit, the soul of a mountain climber, the eye of a lover, the hands of a healer, the compassion of one who sees the whole world as a part of himself. It requires total immersion in the life of Christ and complete concentration on the meaning of the gospel values for a world gone astray.[191]

As spiritual director and retreat giver, Tony Philpot has influenced generations of priests currently in active ministry. He posed the apparently simple question in the late 1990s: 'How do I resource myself for this life?' Based on many years of experience of living as a secular priest and mentoring others, he suggested that it needed 'a mixture of maturity, generosity and awareness'.[192] In an attempt to describe the identity of the secular priest, as lived at the end of the second millennium, Philpot identified certain characteristics. The diocesan priest is a private man, genuinely classless, magisterial, in the sense of speaking on behalf of the authority of the Church. He has to talk, 'far too often' about sacred things, he deals with failure, including his own, and is, at the same time, 'witness to great and miraculous joy among ordinary people'. A diocesan priest has an innate wisdom, learnt of experience.

All of these are the perennial elements of priestly identity, present since the earliest days of the Church, but Philpot went on to pinpoint some of the more uncomfortable aspects of contemporary priesthood: living without a sense of affirmation; a feeling of inadequacy when faced with the particular preoccupations of other priests or laity, such as ecumenism, third world justice, or liturgical correctness; the challenges of a healthy, wholesome life, probably lived alone.[193]

Fundamental to Philpot's sense of the identity of the secular priest was an aspect that has become weakened in recent generations. He was insistent that 'belonging' was vital, by which he meant the relationship that a secular priest has with his diocese. This is a concrete reality to which every priest commits himself at ordination. As a result of social and cultural change, fewer priests by the 1990s, and even fewer in the 2010s, have grown out of the soil of their diocese, in its Catholic families and schools.

Priests enter the presbyterate of their diocese by a wide variety of routes, and what Heenan, in the 1960s, rather cosily called 'an evolving comradeship between priests' has not, for a generation or more, been formed by shared schooling, local culture and common experience of family life. Heenan's assertion that 'holy priests make holy families. Holy families produce priests'[194] looks remote and naïve.

This is not to suggest that diocesan fraternity has become impossible, but that, as Philpot argues,

> We've got to work at it, and be forgiving, both with ourselves and with one another. Ordination is not so much a magic cement, as a motivation for this constant and faithful effort. If we are the kind of people who take offence at the words and deeds of others, and freeze them off for all eternity, our presbyterate does not stand a chance.[195]

This has real significance for priests' appreciation of themselves in history, and of the presbyterate of a diocese being deeply embedded in its local tradition. 'The presbyterate of each diocese has its own characters. It has its own jokes. It has its own collective memories'.[196] One of the real threats to the identity of the secular priesthood and to the fraternity that binds a diocese and expresses the theological identity of the local Church, is the diminution of consciousness of that collective memory, of the history that binds the presbyterate into its own great tradition.

The Costs of Complacency

My brothers! Consider yourselves fortunate when
all sorts of trials come your way, because you know
that when your faith succeeds in facing such trials,
the result is the ability to endure.

(James 1: 2-4)

It may well be true that, by the turn of the millennium, lay deference to clergy had gone, probably for ever, and English Catholics had become,

> Respectable...perhaps they have also become complacent as well as congenitally defensive...Sadly it seems that they have become a rather cosy and unchallengingly domesticated denomination. In this process it seems that the new, younger generations of cradle Catholics have substantially lost an awareness, and hence a pride in their historical roots. There is a weakened sense of a distinctive community evoking a sense of identity and commitment'.[197]

This opinion is coloured by a generational sense of loss. It perhaps reflects a disappointed perspective on what the Council would bring about, based on a view of lay activism that was essentially for the articulate, educated middle class, which was not sure where the priest belonged. This view was also borne out in Desmond Ryan's sociological study of the Archdiocese of

Birmingham, carried out in the 1990s, by means of analysis of interviews with priests and laity.[198] It revisited the negative images developed by Hornsby Smith, and embraced fully the charges of institutional failure, blaming the leadership of the local Church bluntly. The core problem, Ryan asserted, was:

> The inability of the senior levels of the institution to re-absorb inherited structures, evolved in earlier ages for other tasks, into a continuing process of Vatican II-isation, whereby the *opposition* between the Church and the world formerly prevalent is transmuted into a *dialogue* between them.[199]

Ryan glanced at the 'legacy' of history, which he saw as wholly negative, and something to be, in the title of one of his chapters, 'overcome'.[200] His book reflects a casual mind-set that made history an enemy, just at the moment when, ironically, a new generation of mainly Catholic academic historians, were exposing the history of Catholicism in England and Wales to the rigour of professional research and intellectual enquiry. He perpetuated a view that there was an inherited institutional problem, which was an unchanging monolithic Church, incapable of adaptation. A real grasp of the history of English Catholicism shows precisely the opposite, and can be instrumental in strengthening 'a weakened sense of a distinctive community evoking a sense of identity and commitment'.[201]

The more damaging effect of studies such as Ryan and Smith,[202] was to reinforce an institutional view of the future of the local Church, but also, the association of the priesthood with potentially depressive hopelessness. He is, of course, correct in his assertion that 'a self-sufficient priest risks being an inefficient priest',[203] but the use of the word 'inefficient' reflects all the problems inherent in a functional view of priesthood. A priest is not called to give his life to an efficiency campaign. At the end of a discussion that mainly concentrated on structures, ministries and organisation, and on the difficulties and failures inherent in trying to sustain outmoded ones, or introduce new ones, there was, at least, a dawning recognition of what lies at the heart of priestly ministry in the parish.

> Among the people there is a great hunger for a personal experience of God; among many priests there is a great zeal to satisfy that hunger. But to rise to this, as to other

challenges to grow in the Spirit, they must first get rid of
some of the 'guardian of the ghetto' ballast.[204]

Since the time of Ryan's heavy-handed critique, there has begun to be a
more nuanced understanding of what has been going on in parishes over
the last generation, although much elucidation is still needed. A comparison
of the communal response to the celebrations of the centenary of the
restoration of the hierarchy in 1950, and the atmosphere around Pope John
Paul II's visit to England in 1982, Harris suggests, not only reflects changes
in society. It illustrates

> The overarching premium now placed on an experiential,
> self-authenticating and efficacious lived practice which
> might dispense (or sometimes dovetail) with institutional
> expression and hierarchical, clerical determination.[205]

In the years since the millennium, there has been a growing recognition of
the need to challenge the 'weakened sense of a distinctive community'[206]
that Hornsby Smith identified, with numerous initiatives being inspired by
the concept coined by John Paul II of a 'new evangelisation'. There is also
evidence of insecurity about the sort of 'experiential, self-authenticating'
Catholic identity described by Harris and a desire for stronger boundaries
and hierarchies. A number of the younger generation of Catholics have
responded to this in radical ways, which, in some instances, have taken
them into new models of religious life or into new images of priesthood.
Some initiatives have been more fruitful than others. There is still evidence
of confusion in the minds of some of those aspiring to priesthood as to
exactly what vision of ordained ministry they have, and to what it is they
propose to give their lives.

   During this time, there has been significantly less literature on
priesthood, and indeed on Catholic life, emerging from the Church in
England and Wales, with many seminary bookshelves full of the products
of the American experience. While often positive and affirming, it is,
inevitably, shaped by the very different scale and resources, and reflects
the particular conditions of the American Church. It lacks the rootedness in
the history and tradition of the dioceses of England and Wales, which has
shaped priestly identity in this country. The absence of published reflection
on priestly life, written by priests within the local context, suggests a
draining of confidence in expressing what it means to be a secular priest

in this country. It also denies the seminarian the opportunity to grasp a deeper appreciation of the presbyterate to which he aspires to belong.

Much has changed in the priesthood in England and Wales; the declining numbers of identifiable priestly vocations bearing fruit and the abandonment of ministry by younger priests are symptoms, but they are not the causes of the current difficulties. It is surely time to reflect afresh upon what it now means to be a missionary priest in this country, after a quarter of a century of *Pastores Dabo Vobis* and, more especially, in the light of our own history. *Pastores Dabo Vobis* does, after all, suggest that priesthood finds its identity in 'the specific historical and contextual conditions of a particular church'.[207]

Historically, the first half of the mid twentieth century created a mindset, which enabled the Catholic Church in England and Wales to think that it had got things right. It had established a perfect, unchanging pattern of clerical life, and an unstoppable process of physical and numerical growth. A triumphalist view of history convinced English Catholics that continued expansion was possible and achievable without very much strategic thought or effort, and was the mark of the 'success' of the mission. When this apparently unchanging pattern proved not to be so robust, many priests and lay people preferred not to acknowledge it.

The sense of crisis in the present generation is coloured by a received view that the Church of the first half of the twentieth century was the perfect society, on which the optimism and promise of the 1960s was supposed to build, but somehow it all went wrong, and English Catholicism entered a long dark tunnel of decline. This is, quite simply, a false understanding.

> A review of historical data suggests there was never a golden age of Catholics, united, conflict-free, and substantially coerced or socialised into a uniformity of conforming practice and belief by a dominant clergy.[208]

Yet our generation still lives with the belief that this perfect society existed, but it fragmented and was undermined with alarming rapidity in the late twentieth century, leaving a mood of uncertainty and loss of morale. What this has engendered is a nostalgia for something that never actually existed, based on a false understanding of history, and a disinclination to grasp the issues of the day, rather than those of yesterday.

Taking the Past into the Future

I will turn the darkness before them into light, the
rough places into level ground.

(Isaiah 42: 16)

We live in a generation when history is often seen as having little purpose. The televised period drama approach to visiting the past is more popular than ever, but that is part of the leisure and entertainment industry. Understanding and valuing the significance of history is different, and less popular.

There seems to be a problem in western culture at the moment in that it is possible to detect a weariness with history and the notion of being involved in a tradition or stream of continuities throughout time. To base one's life on tradition, or to hark back to the past appears to be a distraction. It is much more common these days for people to believe that 'history' only signifies the past and that the past is what happened rather than something that enables our present to come into being or that invites us to reflect on the future and on what we aspire to.[209]

The speed and complexity of social change, the immediacy of technology, and the fragmentation of traditional communities have, for many people, severed a sense of living connection with the past. This leads either to the rejection described by Sheldrake, or to a fearful and ill-informed retreat into an imagined past of a mythical 'golden age'. The Church is one of the few physical, human and spiritual places in which the living connection with the past remains important. Its history embodies the faith we proclaim, but it becomes an embarrassment when we fail to integrate history into the present and the future.

Every local Church is shaped by its tradition, by its understanding of the history of the people and priests who have sustained it. The experience of the Church in this country, stripped of traditional expressions of faith and ancient institutional structures at the Reformation, together with the struggle to nurture faith and to recreate structures, institutions and buildings, has formed Catholic identity in England and Wales. In particular, it has shaped the identity of its secular priesthood. Without a serious awareness of their historical rootedness, the priests of the present and future face the danger of becoming 'a memory-less culture without a sense of historical identity'.[210]

To a considerable extent, Catholicism in England and Wales has become dislocated from its history, and 'memory-less' in the past couple of generations. In the 1960s and 1970s, there was widespread embarrassment and sensitivity about the canonization of the Forty English Martyrs of the Reformation in 1970, which Cardinal Heenan addressed in a Pastoral Letter:

> The canonisation will not revive religious bitterness. The new-found friendship between Christians will prevent any renewal of old controversies. While we thank God for the glorious memory of our martyrs we do not forget that some Protestants also suffered death for the sake of conscience in the sixteenth century.[211]

For many Catholics, however, the sensitivities were born less out of ecumenical awareness than from a distaste for what seemed to be a whiff of nostalgia for an older, more defensive Church. This 'did not wholly resonate with a 1970s English Catholicism that was ethnically mixed, ecumenically engaged, and focussed on social activism'.[212] That embarrassment embedded itself in the next generation of teachers and priests, for whom the past was monolithic and inhibiting. It is echoed in Desmond Ryan's dismissal, in the 1990s, of history as a legacy to be overcome.[213]

History struggled to find a place in seminary formation, and the history of English Catholicism was rarely taught in Catholic schools. This created a generation of Catholics, largely convinced that nothing fruitful could be gained from a consideration of the history of the Church. This has impoverished the understanding of ourselves within the life of the local Church, and weakened communal identity and mission. It is timely to remind ourselves, as Pope Francis did in a 2015 homily, that service and mission flow from a sense of history, from 'being men and women of history, by understanding that the story does not begin or end with me'.[214]

The Reformation took the secular priests from the heart of medieval parochial society, transforming them into missionaries. Those priests had to face the unthinkable dissolution of Catholicism in these lands, and take the initiative to turn loss and destruction into creativity and new life. Many roots were torn up in the sixteenth century, leaving new traditions and a new culture to grow within the Established Church. The secular priests, newly designated as missionaries, had to give form to the re-emergent Catholic community. The ways in which that came about, in turn reshaped the identity of the secular priesthood.

The path from medieval religious culture to missionary Catholicism created an intimacy, and sense of a shared purpose between the priests and the laity who supported and enabled them. Throughout most of the post-Reformation period it was rare for a priest to have a settled home and church from which to minister to a geographically identifiable group of people. The scale of Catholic life in its new missionary form meant that local knowledge, family networks, strong local presence and, above all, personal commitment were vital.

Post-Reformation secular priests lived, for generations, in relative isolation from each other and from the small number of bishops, having to generate their own energy. They had to evolve new ways of life, different forms of leadership and alternative ways of relating to the structures of the Church. They had to respond to a wide variety of dynamics within the Catholic community, in a rapidly changing society. The direction and momentum has without fail, been local, stimulated by local conditions, and not in response to a master plan for a district, diocese or national Church. This has embedded within the priesthood a distinctive culture of localism, pragmatism and missionary enterprise.

The specific historical identity of secular priests came firstly from being outlaws and refugees in their own country, producing from among their own number, martyrs and victims of oppressive state legislation. Once the period of immediate personal danger was over, priests in England were still a tiny and isolated group, living in a land, at best indifferent, at worst hostile, to its activities and maintained by a Catholic laity with whom relations could be complicated. Relationships were nurtured in the creation of safe houses, in the provision of property where none existed, in charitable giving, fund raising and supporting the building and provision of churches, schools and other institutions.

In the nineteenth century, the role of the priesthood within the Catholic community was transformed, as priests began to exercise authority over a larger and more structured organization. Missionary priests became entrepreneurs and professional specialists in pastoral leadership. As parishes eventually became a reality, the priests moved to the centre of that expression of Catholic life. The newly built churches, and particularly the presbyteries, became different and privileged spaces, part of the mystique associated with priesthood.

There were many attempts to create a separate and distinctive Catholic culture, which was bolstered by migration and conversion. That changed, when tight Catholic parish identities began to disperse in the post-1945 redevelopment of Britain's cities. The second half of the twentieth century witnessed shifts in social and political attitudes to authority, especially where it touched people's personal lives. The authoritative expert, including the parish priest, was no longer automatically obeyed, and a mood of uncertainty about the identity of the priest settled upon both clergy and laity.

Since the Reformation, Catholics in this country have constantly learned to embrace radical and frequent change, and to adapt to meet new challenges. Just as in the past, priests today face a need to embrace previously unthinkable change in the nature of the communities they lead, together with the possibilities of a new and radically different future. As much as at any point in the last five hundred years, the courageous and imaginative leadership of the missionary secular priesthood is needed now. A reappraisal of traditional ways, found in our history, must be open to the possibilities of real change in our own time.

The death of old certainties takes place at particular moments in history; the phase inaugurated in the 1560s was one such moment, and our own generation is another. The cultural, social and religious transformation under way in our own time is as profound and far reaching as that of the Reformation. Fresh consideration of the changing nature of Catholic communities and parishes in the past and present is needed, in order to build for the future; our history tells us that managed decline is not the only option.

Facing and embracing change, trusting in God's providence, clearing pathways, and offering opportunities to look afresh at the world around and discern a new relationship with it, can be a powerful means of renewal. Care and attentiveness is needed over what is retained, what can be salvaged, and what should be consigned to the past. The preservation of tradition is different from holding onto what is merely habitual and familiar. In defining the future, as part of the process of evolving a new vision and creating a new order, certainties are shaken. During the present times of transition for the priesthood, the past can illuminate the present; it can help to identify and prepare for the transitions of our own day. History can be harnessed to power renewal.

The rest of this book contains reflection on some of the themes that emerge from an exploration of history, which continue to resonate in the lives of priests today. Three aspects of priestly life are considered: how the individual priest lives his life, how he relates to his brother priests and bishops, and how he leads the community placed in his care. Contemporary English priestly identity is shaped by the efforts of previous generations to address these issues. No generation had perfect solutions, and each one faced fresh difficulties and possibilities. The search for solutions shaped their identity and that of the Church in this country. The rediscovery of the unique qualities of priestly identity in the Church in England and Wales can be the basis for the future.

The present cannot be divorced from the past, and the past always bears the seeds of the future...As if living in the present and reverencing one's tradition were not sufficiently complex, then, leaders must, above all commit to creating the future of their organisations and communities. Here's how Pope Francis once described the delicate interplay of past, present and future that the leader must balance: "Memory of our roots, courage in the face of the unknown, capturing the reality of the moment." Pope Francis will fail ignominiously if all he manages to do is to embrace the present and preserve his tradition as an unchanging, static museum piece.[215]

Priestly Life or Clerical Life?

See that I follow not the wrong path, and lead me in the path of life eternal.

(Psalm 138: 24)

Consideration of the identity of the individual priest calls for reflection on the ways in which a priest understands himself and his vocation. It requires an honest answer to the question: priestly identity or clerical identity – what is the difference? Priestly identity embodies authority, personal integrity and the integration of a man's personality in his own self-awareness as a priest. Clerical identity is about power. 'A cleric is someone who attempts to be a priest from the outside in. He assumes and adopts the uniform, behaviour and language of the institution. Ultimately, even his perception and thought become institutionalised'.[216] O'Leary called for an open and honest recognition of clericalism and a debate about it, in order for priests to better fulfil 'the real, urgent, God-given mission for the Church and for the world today'.[217] That honest recognition is still needed, perhaps even more than when those words were written twenty years ago.

In the constrained, ordered, limited life of obedience and duty inflicted on priests for a large portion of the twentieth century, there was no choice but to inhabit an imposed model. Only a rigid exercise of obedience enabled priests to cope with externally imposed change. They were inhibited in their personal growth in self-knowledge, and therefore in continuing discernment and openness to change. Consideration of the clerical identity imposed on priests in the first part of the twentieth century suggests how difficult it can be to contemplate anything different. If the identity is clerical rather than priestly, then professional 'busyness' gets in the way of an inner awareness of needs. Thomas Carlyle suggested that it was better to die of exhaustion than boredom, yet both can be lethal; exhaustion can be the fruit of compulsive, fruitless busyness, while boredom can produce *ennui* and depression.

No priest should be expected to fit a model or conform to one; he is the man God has called to priesthood in his individual humanity, and he has his own path of priesthood to tread. He is not called to a 'model' of priesthood. In fact, the use of the word 'model' in relation to priesthood is unhelpful, and should really be abandoned. Every priest needs to take responsibility for the shape of his own priesthood. Only then is it possible for priests to contemplate honestly the nature, extent, and possibility of change, for themselves and others.

In order to do so, priests must be free from fears that keep them locked into unhealthy attachments to the familiar and habitual, or to inherited notions of status. That freedom can be destroyed by taking on structural limitations and inhibitions that starve it to death.

Discernment of a priestly vocation takes a man considerable time and effort on the journey towards seminary, and during the years of initial formation. It may be assumed that, once the bishop lays his hands on a man's head, and seals him in a lifelong commitment to priesthood, that discernment is over. In reality, a priest, like anyone else, faces a lifetime journey towards fuller and deeper personal integration. This requires continued discernment about how a truly priestly life is to be lived.

A priest needs to become conscious of his own needs and find the means to fulfil them, in order to be able to help others do the same. The fundamental needs lie in his relationship with God, the quality of which must be nurtured by constant prayer, spiritual direction, retreats and spiritual reading and the celebration of the sacraments with and for the people of God. All of these resources are necessary to support and nourish a life of prayer. It is, however, only in the silence of the desert that they are all stripped away, leaving only the presence of God. The busier the life, the more need there is for time in the desert, to focus on what lies at the core of our being.[218] A priest should not, indeed cannot avoid the desert, whatever form it might take. It is, paradoxically, a place of growth.

The desert was inflicted on the priests of the Recusant period, who were forced to be self-reliant in prayer and to nourish themselves in lives of isolation, fear and lack of support. They had to take responsibility for their own spiritual wellbeing. The desert is a place where horizons may be glimpsed. It is only really possible to see the horizon from an open, unprotected place, from an edge, a mountain top or a sea shore. The generations of priests who lived without walls and without shelter recognized this. They acknowledged both the paralysing fear and the energising hope that a distant horizon can engender.

William Allen looked towards a distant horizon, sending men to uncertain lives and possible death, trusting only in God's providence to prevent the tiny English mission from flickering and dying. Richard Challoner, two centuries later, as missionary priest and bishop, lived in the desert of a series of anonymous rented rooms in central London, never having a fixed address or an altar at which to celebrate Mass, yet he prophesied 'a new people', not knowing what lay ahead. Wherever the desert is found, it is the starting place from where each individual priest sets his feet towards a new horizon, trusting in God and in God's people.

Isolation became an established pattern among Recusant priests. They also had to find the means to care for themselves, to supply their own food, drink and personal health and well-being, dealing with independence and isolation. This became institutionalised to an unhealthy degree, long regarded as the proper pattern of clerical life. The twentieth century diplomat and philosopher, Dag Hammarskjöld is quoted as saying: 'Pray that your loneliness may spur you into finding something to live for, great enough to die for'. That concept might inspire, but it carries danger. The damaging effects of loneliness are now increasingly recognised in modern society as outcomes of growing individualism and the fragmentation of traditional families and communities. The priest's journey is individual but not solitary, and isolation is unhealthy.

The Church continues to believe and to teach that celibacy is intrinsic to priesthood; therefore, it is difficult to separate discourse about priestly identity from discussion of celibacy. When fully lived and embraced, priestly celibacy can be a source of inner dynamism, freeing men to consecrate themselves for God's service. It can also trap priests into self-imposed expectations of constant availability. Celibacy should not mean an absence of life-giving and honest relationships. If that is the reality, then priesthood is dishonest, and in danger of becoming clericalism – lived from the outside in. The illusion of self-sufficiency is the poison of the celibate life. It means that nobody is there to say the good and encouraging things, and the more uncomfortable ones, that priests need to hear and understand about themselves.

Loneliness was part of a pattern of priestly life for many missionary priests in England and Wales after the Reformation. It was, at times, unavoidable for the priest moving across country under cover, or living an awkward 'between stairs' life in a gentry household. When a healthy solution to loneliness was found, it was most likely to be in a domestic household. Individual priests have left scant evidence of their lives, but it must be assumed that the likelihood of unhealthy close relationships was considerable. Cardinal Philip Howard believed that excessively close contact between priests and women was one of the dangers that could be alleviated by the adoption of a clerical fraternity. He understood the importance of responsible human relationships to the psychological, physical and spiritual health of priests.

One way in which all relationships can become irresponsible is if they depend on one-way communication. No-one can be held responsible for the way in which another person receives a message, but if it conveys more than simple information, it risks being a reflection of dominance, control and lack of responsiveness. This is an increasing danger with electronic communication, although it is just as possible on parish noticeboards. The announcement on a website, email, social media or notice board demands attention and response, but it does not invite participation. What is within the individual, waiting to be drawn out, cannot be reached in one-way communication. Conversation matters, and recent research suggests that, without it, individuals can easily develop a lack of empathy.

Careful monitoring of dependence on electronic media, insistence on the maintenance of personal communication, on the importance of conversation is becoming increasingly vital for all of us. The delicate relationships that bind priests and people together in communion can become weakened and confused without care and attention. Priests may find themselves among the few people who continue to understand the profound importance of conversation, so it is important that they do not forget the art.

> Human relationships are rich, messy and demanding. When we clean them up with technology, *we move from conversation to the efficiencies of mere connection.* I fear we forget the difference. And we forget that children who grow up in a world of digital devices don't know that there is a difference, or that things were ever different.[219]

Priests need to be able to live differently. This may or may not mean that they live alone, and may or may not mean that they themselves are lonely. Living alone does not need to mean loneliness, and living with others is not necessarily a solution to loneliness and its consequences. Aloneness does not need to be fed, but can be used creatively as a space in which to engage with culture and civilization. It requires of all people, but especially of priests, an inner journey from loneliness to solitude, to creativity. The fear of silence and space, which, instead of being an opportunity for exploration, gets filled with busyness, is lethal.

Withdrawal from the possibility of exploration and creativity is a sign of emptiness and decline, and can be a response to the stifling effect of being in a rut, or in a barren environment. There is a need to recognise the imperative to change the environment; something that can rarely be done alone, yet it does require solitude. Time spent on the internet is not solitude, and communication by text, tweet or mobile phone is not conversation. 'We slip into thinking that always being connected is going to make us less lonely. But we are at risk that it is actually the reverse: if we are unable to be alone, we will be more lonely'.[220] The costs of withdrawal and isolation can be extremely high, for the individual and for those around him. 'It's the capacity for solitude that allows you to reach out to others and see them as separate and independent'.[221]

Abuse, in all its forms, of power, sex, alcohol, food or drugs, is most likely to occur at times of stress, loneliness, and isolation. Such stressful or challenging situations trigger the desire in some priests to form inappropriate and dangerous relationships. Other routes lie in excessive or inappropriate reliance on internet contacts, compulsive use of food, drink or other substances. Access to ongoing human formation, to the kind of help that empowers an individual to understand his environment, and to discern the need to change it, especially at times when priests are most vulnerable, is now being more readily appreciated. It would seem to be beneficial in all sorts of ways, to individuals, and to the wider Church. It could also be one step towards reducing the likelihood of all forms of abuse in future generations. Recognising the reality of the dangers of isolation, and learning the gift of solitude is crucial for human and spiritual wellbeing.

True civilization, it has been suggested, is closely connected with spiritual wellbeing, and is constituted by the quality of our relationships with ideas, objects and people. 'One of the central ideas of civilization is that people might be persuaded, not by fear, but by joy'.[222] The persuasiveness of the joy of the Gospel is a message that Pope Francis has made the theme of his papacy. Spiritual wellbeing is the source of the profound joy, the 'true civilization' without which priests of any generation cannot function.

Priestly Fraternity: a Source of Grace

Keep on loving those who know you, doing justice
for upright hearts.
(Psalm 35: 11)

I t is surely right that care for fellow priests is a duty and a responsibility, not simply a human one, but a sacramental one. It is a source of grace.[223] The silence of mistrust and enclosure needs to be broken by hospitality and real fraternity, by creating safe places where real conversation is possible. Finding the momentum, and making the safe places for conversation that may change minds and hearts is a sign of real human maturity.

> Conversation is a meeting of minds with different memories and habits. When minds meet, they don't just exchange facts: they transform them, reshape them, draw different implications from them, engage in new trains of thought. Conversation doesn't just reshuffle the cards: it creates new cards.[224]

The fraternity of the secular priesthood is part of the tradition of the Church in this country, uniquely shaped by local circumstances, but it is in need of restoration. It involves willingness to have real adult conversations, between men who have shared similar experiences of vocation, seminary formation and priestly life, rather than retreating into received clerical models. Renewing the fraternity of the secular priesthood is essential, in order to help more priests to move out of a competitive, at best indifferent, even hostile response to brother priests. Competition between priests is prevalent, and dangerous, especially competitive busyness, in which one believes himself to be busier, more in demand, more needed, more sought out than his neighbour. Effective fraternal conversation does not inhibit, threaten or intimidate, but makes it possible to overcome fears of revealing personal limitations.

Philpot developed this theme, with disarming simplicity:

> "Fraternity" isn't a mysterious code word which conveys a message to the uninitiated. We are not freemasons. It means no more, no less, than being friends. How odd it is that in the Church we can be so many other things. Rulers, servants, teachers, pupils, apprentices, experts, preachers – and in all these ways we enter into relationship with one another. But the most precious of all relationships is friendship; inside it, you can speak the truth to one another with love. It is a quality that should infect all our dealings.[225]

The fathers of the Second Vatican Council insisted on the value of priestly fraternity. They encouraged hospitality, kindness, generosity and shared recreation among priests, with particular care for those who are struggling, coping with illness, or who are lonely or in difficulties. *Presbyterorum Ordinis* explicitly stated that:

> In order that priests may find mutual assistance in the development of their spiritual and intellectual life, that they may be able to cooperate more effectively in their ministry and be saved from the dangers of loneliness which may arise, it is necessary that some kind of common life or some sharing of common life be encouraged among priests.[226]

The Council's teaching was incorporated in the 1983 *Code of Canon Law*, which expressed 'esteem' for associations that promote 'fraternal assistance' and the 'unity of clerics among themselves and with their own bishop'.[227] It 'highly recommends' the practice of some form of common life,[228] and encouraged seminaries to instill in seminarians a sense of 'fraternal union with the diocesan *presbyterium* whose partners they will be in the service of the Church'. [229] Both *Pastores Dabo Vobis* in 1992 and the *Directory on the Life and Ministry of Priests* in 1994 reiterated the same message. *Pastores Dabo Vobis* insisted forcefully that it is 'impossible not to recommend' forms of common life among priests, not only as a means of support to priests in their ministry, but as 'a shining example of charity and unity'.[230] How much more effective the preaching of charity and unity is, when those preaching are also living it out.

Fraternity is embedded in the local church of the diocese into which a priest is incardinated, and his sharing with the bishop in the care of the people in a specific historical and cultural setting.[231] All of the recent teaching documents of the Church reinforce the importance of the diocesan identity of the secular priesthood, which is not merely accidental, but is rooted in the history and tradition of a specific area. Belonging as a diocesan priest has a very particular quality, reflecting the fraternity of the presbyterate, but it needs to be nurtured and sustained. Ordination does not automatically create fraternity. The *Directory on the Life and Ministry of Priests* (1994) expressed a strong sense of communion between priests and bishop in the local church, which, 'besides being an expression of maturity... contributes to the building of that unity in the communion which is indispensable for the work of evangelization'. It called on the priest to live out the communion that he preaches.[232]

In a particular way, this is emphasized in the identity of the secular priest in relation to the diocese to which he belongs. The *Directory* points out that every priest is a member of a specific presbyterate, and that there are 'no theological foundations' for the idea of a universal priesthood.[233] It makes the point that priestly fraternity is not an option, but is inherent in the sacramental identity of priesthood.

> Priestly fraternity and membership to a presbyterate are, therefore, elements characterizing the priest. The rite of the imposition of the hands by the Bishop and all of the priests present during the priestly ordination has special significance and merit, because it points to the equality of participation in the ministry, and to the fact that the priest cannot act by himself; he acts within the presbyterate, becoming a brother of all those who constitute it.[234]

A bishop and the priests of his diocese owe it to each other to give time and attention to their relationship, to the development of real friendship, of mature relationships of mutual support and encouragement, of honesty and integrity. It can be difficult, but is not impossible, even given what Tony Philpot has called the anarchic streak in priests. The influence of the lack of contact with authentic leadership and authority is reflected in the history of English priesthood. The battles over episcopal leadership and authority eventually bore fruit in the dominant characters that appeared after 1850, with their new found office, but all too rarely the personal qualities with which to fulfil it. Bishops became remote authority figures and a Catholic reflection of Victorian paternalism. It may be timely to ask what a mature relationship between priest and bishop looks like, and to insist that it requires deliberate attention.

The difficulty faced in the present time is that rootedness in a diocese has become weakened in recent generations, due to a variety of factors, including a lack of awareness of the history and tradition of the diocese. This is partly due to the educational weaknesses of previous generations, but not entirely. The historical locations and buildings, and local saints, the legendary characters, the stories of bishops long gone are all important in sustaining a sense of diocesan identity. The presbyterate of a diocese has a profound need to understand its foundational history, but also to appreciate its myths and heroes, and a conscious determination to imbibe the history and tradition is important. There are social and religious factors that make this a fundamental and urgent need, rather than merely desirable.

Increased mobility for work or study, or personal choice means that a larger proportion of priests offer themselves to dioceses where they have little sense of rootedness, and scant awareness of its traditions. Many priests come from families where Catholic faith is weak, or have no religious affiliation, so they have entered the priesthood as adult converts to Catholicism. Cardinal Heenan's catchphrase that 'Holy priests make holy families. Holy families produce priests' seemed quaint even in the 1960s, but is rarely true today. Priests bring their upbringing and background into their priesthood, and it is often not an experience of the sort of 'holy family' envisaged by Heenan that was familiar in earlier generations. For many, therefore, imbibing the history and identity of Catholicism in England and Wales demands real effort and engagement.

Priestly diocesan fraternity is not accidental; it requires conscious and deliberate building up. For the last twenty years and more, former Anglican clergy have joined dioceses, often bringing wives and families with them. One of the challenges for them is to embrace the Catholic understanding of diocesan 'belonging' and to gain an appreciation of the history and tradition of the diocese to which they now belong. Short spells in seminary cannot always help them to achieve this. The diocesan presbyterate who share a sense of communal identity, having spent years together in discernment, formation and ministry, have a responsibility to evoke the traditions of the diocese in ways that enable new arrivals to appreciate it and to enter fully into it.

The same is true, to an even greater extent, in relation to the overseas priests who have entered dioceses for longer or shorter periods of time, whose identity is shaped by different cultures. They bolster the presbyteral numbers, and often bring fresh energy and vision to parishes, but they too are challenged by their unfamiliarity with the culture and identity of the diocese into which they are welcomed. Integration into the communal identity and fraternity of the local priesthood can be difficult for them to achieve. It is a responsibility of their new brother priests to find ways in which diocesan traditions can be shared, and be open to ways in which different experiences of priestly identity can contribute to the next chapter of the history of a diocese and the constant evolution of the local Church.

Recent decades have also witnessed an enhanced permanent diaconate in virtually every diocese in the country; they are frequently drawn from the local parish communities and are likely to have a strong sense of local identity. It is not unusual for them to have a stronger appreciation of their local roots than the priests with whom they work. They are beginning to forge their own communal history and identity as a diaconal community. Parishioners are still, however, often confused about their role in relation to that of the priest. This can serve to undermine lay appreciation and understanding of priestly identity, and also weaken the quality and depth of priestly identity within the priesthood itself.

The typical priests in parishes of even thirty years ago, the local men, bred in the soil of their home diocese, are now relatively rare. The common tradition of seminary priests, who spent at least six years together in formation, and had often been at junior seminary or local

Catholic schools together is less in evidence than in the past. The mix of background and education, the later age of entry to seminary and shorter tailored programmes of formation all tend to weaken what is already a waning tradition. All of the men called to ordained ministry have a part to play in the conversation about the diocesan fraternity and identity of secular priesthood in our own times. Without this, the likelihood of nurturing native vocations to the secular priesthood in the parishes of England and Wales will continue to decline.

The history and traditions of English seminaries have had a powerful effect on the identity of secular priests and the nature of English Catholicism. The martyr tradition of the overseas colleges was powerful and still retains influence, although the number of colleges representing that tradition is depleted. The enclosed, quasi-monastic discipline that became characteristic of English seminaries between the middle of the nineteenth century and the late twentieth century built on the earlier traditions of self-reliance and independence. It bred, at its worst, a priesthood incapable of knowing itself or the people to whom it ministered, unless individuals broke out of the straitjacket. At its best, it created a powerful sense of communal identity.

The 'seedbed' image associated with the concept of seminaries since the sixteenth century, may have been overplayed and outlived its value. Men who enter seminary now are generally not the boys, the 'seedlings', envisaged in the Tridentine model. The 'seedbed' suggests a random and hopeful scattering of seed, expecting some to flourish and others not. A better image for the formation of the priesthood of the present and future is that of an orchard or plantation. If we plant a tree, we do not expect more trees, but a stronger, more fruitful tree, as it is fed and nurtured. Other trees can flourish in its shade, although too many large trees can choke fresh growth and cast a deep shadow over young saplings. Seminarians preparing for the Church of the future need to be like trees, of different growth habits, of various shapes, colours and heights, individually planted, and requiring long term support and nurture. Seminary formation staff and bishops do not need to be gardeners, sifting the weeds from the seeds, but arboriculturalists, supporting, pruning and training stronger trees. The work is continuous.

The newly ordained in Recusant times were prepared for the transition to ministry by taking the missionary oath, being advised to put on a convincing disguise and find their way discreetly to a friendly Catholic house or fellow priest. Not all made it. From the large institutions of the nineteenth and twentieth centuries, they were cast on the mercies, gentle or otherwise, of their first parish priest, and told to behave themselves. It is now increasingly widely recognised that the transition between seminary and parish life requires a little more than that. Integration between seminary and ministry can only be achieved by a recognition that what applied in the past should not be uncritically perpetuated. The Church cannot afford priestly formation for the past, rather like armies always said to be trained to win the last war. Formation needs to be geared towards the horizon, towards a future as yet uncharted.

The life of the seminary can nurture a sense of identity and belonging, but it can also nurture learned patterns of behaviour, which, when passed on, can create characteristics but not true identity. Conforming to others' ready-made thoughts and ways leads to lethargy, and a gap between outward show and inner emptiness, so that the individual becomes a shadow of a person, not thinking through the meaning of his actions, or the effects of them. A missionary priest in the future needs to be capable of thinking for himself, and, where necessary, ditching the ideas of those around him. This was the choice faced in the 1560s, when conformity was the obvious course to follow, and Recusancy took extraordinary courage.

The Priest in the Parish: Shopkeeper or Sherpa?

*Let us then pursue what makes for peace and
for mutual upbuilding.*

(Romans 14: 19)

S cripture gives us the image of servant leadership from Jesus himself
and his disciples. It speaks of a shared and supportive life, a life of
communion.

> Communion living affirms the value of individuals and the
> encouragement of each person's potential for good; the
> fostering of reciprocal relationships of interdependence;
> willingness to see "the other" as one's brother or sister;
> and collaboration rather than unhealthy competition.[235]

Robert K Greenleaf, the guru of servant leadership in the secular world,
described it as leadership that has its focus on the growth and wellbeing of
people and the communities to which they belong. Other people's needs
and priorities are served by this philosophy of leadership exercised within
an institution.[236] The servant leadership exercised by the priest must
have purpose and direction; simply 'keeping the show on the road' is not

enough. To call people fully into the mission of the Church is to help them to move from the place they are in, to somewhere more open to God's grace. The most prominent example in today's Church and world is that of Pope Francis, who frequently uses the language of servant leadership, and criticises leaders who dominate or control.

The laity is inherently a volunteer body, which constantly makes choices, as it has done throughout history. The changing composition and behaviour of the laity require serious, honest reflection. Challenges lie in making new relationships. In some places, new cultural and spiritual influences are brought to bear, often by recently settled migrant communities. In others, a plummeting number of Mass attenders, and of people willing to commit time and energy is rendering the mission almost impossible. The fundamental question that faces priests in parishes, as it has done for generations, is how to understand the reality of people's lives and work with the grain rather than against it. If the relationships between priests and people are fractured, this leads to a lack of trust and respect on both sides. If parishioners feel let down, unheard, misunderstood and not led, they will no longer continue to show up and put up.

For too long, English Catholicism has been obsessed with numbers. The Recusant priests had to work by encountering the people in front of them, and risking rejection or worse, but much of the history has been written in terms of success or failure. The questions too often have been: how many were won back to the Church, how many priests were ordained, how many received the sacraments, attended Catholic schools, how much was in the bank account, how many churches could be built, and so on. This obsession with numbers paralysed the Church, and falsely defined the mission. It created a deep-seated and corrosive attachment to an idea that the history of post-Reformation Catholicism has been one of constant numerical and institutional expansion followed by sudden and inexplicable collapse. It is not surprising that this has created a mood of failure and depression.

There is an urgent need to change our language from that of growth or decline, based simply on head counts, and to examine the depth and quality of the encounter with Christ that people are offered. It does not take mass action to change things, but a small number of passionate and committed people to influence the world around us. The rebirth of the English Church was not the result of a mass movement, but a small-scale, local enterprise, designed to transform timid or careless Catholics into conscientious and courageous witnesses.[237] The quality of faith, life, witness and relationships count for more than quantity.

Between about 1850 and 1950, the Church in England and Wales laboured to bring to fruition plans for churches, schools and parochial institutions, of which it became justly proud. Among them were the thousands of parish churches and presbyteries, which enforced a shape, even an identity, not only on parishes but on priests themselves. The presbytery can be both a sheltering haven of peace and privacy and an isolating retreat from social contact. It can be a place of fraternal welcome and hospitality and a bleak, functional workplace. It can be, for the laity, both a welcoming resort and an impenetrable fortress. The priest can be, both literally and metaphorically, locked in. If the buildings have become a clerical space rather than a priestly space, this inhibits priests from helping people to see the buildings for what they really are.

The nineteenth and twentieth centuries built for certainty, for permanence in one location, reflecting a misplaced understanding and attachment to the medieval past. People will express loyalty to buildings and structures, but the priestly task is to enable people to see what is important and not important about them. Neglect or indifference robs people of their culture, history and identity, of their civilisation. The buildings created in past generations have strong local and personal associations and are, therefore, difficult to see as dispensable or redundant. Priests who are locked into churches and presbyteries will find it impossible to lead their parishioners into a new land, or at least encourage them to think beyond the walls. Mission without buildings was effective for centuries in this country, but this generation needs a different kind of courage, in order to make the choices that release both priests and people from over-dependence on buildings.

Defining what a parish is has become more difficult. There are those who suggest that a 'consumerist' or supermarket mindset has taken root in attitudes to parishes.[238] The image that fits the situation in England and Wales is not that of the supermarket, but that of the corner shop. Our generation has inherited a situation in which we have a large number of 'corner shops' manned by a priest who keeps it 'Open All Hours'. It is assumed that the priest will be constantly available to meet the demands of people at times that are convenient to them. He may provide a service that, like the occasional pint of milk, is grudgingly paid for and only spasmodically required. Yet, like the corner shopkeeper, he continues to provide this service on his own terms, at his own prices, and, it must be said, at times, somewhat reluctantly. It may be stretching the analogy too far, but perhaps there is a lesson in the very recent cultural phenomenon of the recovery and reinvention of the corner shop or village shop, as a communal enterprise, in which all share responsibility and investment.

The parish is, of course, much more than a community shop, and its purpose reaches into the depths of people's hearts and to the heights of their striving to live fully human lives in the presence of God. The image of the priest as the corner shopkeeper, feeding an occasional demand for services, might be replaced by something more like a Sherpa, who leads mountaineers through risky and uncharted territory to undreamed of heights. The people led by the Sherpa-priest are committed and purposeful about scaling the mountain, but need the unique and special gifts of the leader who has the intimate familiarity of the territory that is God. This will only become more than fantasy if there is a genuine recognition that the future has to be different, not worse than the present or past, and that we all have to go there.

Pope Francis, at the celebration of the fiftieth anniversary of the Synod of Bishops, called passionately for 'a synodal Church' at every level, for 'a Church which listens, which realizes that listening "is more than simply hearing" (*Evangelii Gaudium*, 171). It is a mutual listening in which everyone has something to learn'.[239] Soon after that, he went even further in developing this theme at a synod of the Italian Church:

> In a special way, I also recommend to you the capacity to dialogue and to encounter. To dialogue is not to negotiate. To negotiate is to try to take one's "slice" of the common cake. This is not what I mean, but it is to seek the common good for all. Discuss together, I dare say get angry together, think of the best solutions for all. Many times a meeting is involved in conflict. There is conflict in dialogue: it is logical and foreseeable that it be so. And we must not fear it or ignore it, but accept it. We must accept "to endure the conflict, to resolve it and to transform it into a ring of connection of a new process" (*Evangelii Gaudium*, 227).[240]

The parish is the place of encounter with the culture of our secular world, which needs compassion, mercy, patience and love. Just as much as the Recusants were exiles in their own land, waiting for signs of God's providence, we are exiles. We need to remind ourselves that there is no other place for us to sing the song of the Lord. This is our time and our place, where God has planted us. Recusant writings are not suffused with self-pity for the troublesome times and the threats they faced, but with a determined sense of mission in reality. Perhaps 'mission in reality' is the motto for 2016 and beyond.

'A race whom the Lord has blessed'

You shall dwell in the land which I gave to your fathers:
and you shall be my people and I will be your God.

(Ezekiel 36: 28)

Fix your gaze on the mission, the vision, the goal that ultimately draws and inspires; and then make yourself free to race after it, free from anything that might hold you back. Be free. Be free from whatever internal baggage and attachments might hold you back or cloud your judgement. Be free for sound, bold, inspired choices that serve the mission and lead it forward.[241]

In order to make 'sound, bold, inspired choices', continued discernment is needed in priestly life. That discernment is not about the fundamental decision to answer God's call to priesthood. It is about the things that block the vision and inhibit the freedom to serve the mission in the future, not in the past. Continued exploration and growth in self-knowledge is the foundation on which effective priesthood is built. It is in this place that imagination resides; the power to imagine 'the other', the possibilities of transformation. Without imagination, true priestliness is lost and becomes functional, leading to clericalism.

The message from our history is that it was the secular priests who became missionaries, and built a new future by making sound, bold and inspired decisions. They also made mistakes. Missionary priests were inspired to take risks, and to be reshaped by the lessons learned. They are called to do so again. These are not the risks of imprisonment and torture, of ostracism and homelessness, but the risks of accepting mature leadership. The risks are those of the Sherpa, who is willing to lead, knowing that everyone is tied together. We enable each other to climb higher, or pull each other down into a crevasse. The post-Reformation mission in England and Wales demonstrates the power of a network of interdependence, without which the local Church in this country would not have survived or flourished. Priests were sustained by the networks of laity who supported, protected and nurtured them in so many ways, often unrecorded in history. This interdependence is an essential part of our present experience, which must be understood, accepted and, indeed, revered by every priest and lay person today. Mission requires of the secular priesthood the courage and inspiration to respond to change, to lead people through it and to respect and recognise that the mission is not a clerical one. A truly priestly mission is created, shared and built in the relationships between priests and people.

Throughout our history, growth and new life have not come from elaborate structural plans but from individual courage and insight, and from local initiatives. New possibilities will only emerge out of a strengthened identity among priests and a re-imagining of leadership, enabling hope and trust to be renewed among priests and laity. This generation has the capacity to enlarge our vision of what the presence of the Church can mean in our time. It means more than 'running a parish', stretching priests to an extent that militates against real priestly presence. When the priest becomes functional rather than inspirational, he damages himself, individuals and communities. It is in the complex network of relationships, of mutual dependence that the secular priest belongs and where he becomes fully alive and finds his true vocation.

Supported by a recovery of the great tradition of the secular priesthood we can embark on a fresh chapter of our history, led by a body of priests renewed in confidence and ready to look forward and embrace the unfamiliar. Like our Recusant forebears, we all need fresh incentive to 'put out into the deep', and to make the spiritual and pastoral choices that enable priests to lead people through uncharted territory. Priesthood is not the place for ambition or competitiveness, for scoring numbers, building structures or achieving position. The measure of its fruitfulness is the faith of other people, and their capacity to bear witness to Christ.

Parish structures are changing before our eyes, and challenging the identity of the parish priest evolved over the past five hundred years, and embedded in the structures we have created. Pope Francis has recently suggested that 'we are not in an era of change, but in a change of era'.[242] The Catholic Church in England and Wales in this 'change of era' is experiencing a cultural transformation more profound than anything since the Reformation. It is time again for the secular priesthood to step forward and respond to the exalted, exciting and demanding call made on them.

These final reflections upon the historical and contemporary identity of the secular priesthood in England and Wales are being written in Passiontide and Holy Week. As I consider the possible relevance of these ideas to the future of the secular priesthood in this country, I am inspired by a tiny detail, which is found in St John's account of the Crucifixion. It is drawn to our attention, almost as an afterthought, but it is central to the meaning of Jesus' death:

> When the soldiers had finished crucifying Jesus they took his clothing and divided it into four shares, one for each soldier. His undergarment was seamless, woven in one piece from neck to hem; so they said to one another, 'Instead of tearing it, let's throw dice to decide who is to have it'. In this way the words of scripture were fulfilled; *'They shared out my clothing among them. They cast lots for my clothes.'* (John 19: 23-4)

The seamless garment is analogous to the garment of the High Priest, mentioned in the Old Testament, as a sign of Jesus fulfilling his role as High Priest, in offering himself as the sacrifice. Jesus is the perfect High Priest who opens the way for all to enter into the presence of God by offering the perfect sacrifice for the sins of the world. He is both the sacrificial victim and the priest offering the sacrifice; this passage takes us to the heart of what Good Friday means.

The image of the seamless garment takes us straight to the most intimate and vivid moment of Jesus' suffering, and connects the sacrifice offered by every priest at the altar to the sacrifice of Jesus, the High Priest. It speaks of the absolute and unique intimacy between the priest and the suffering of Jesus. The seamless garment is the last thing stripped away from Jesus by his torturers, revealing his complete, broken humanity. It was almost certainly not the pristine garment portrayed in much religious art. It would, by the time he reached Golgotha, have stuck to his body with sweat, blood, spittle and tears, caked in dust, and was probably already worn, torn and damaged from three years on the road.

The priesthood finds its meaning in the union between Christ and his Church, so the continuity of priesthood, which has been the subject of this study, bears witness to the fact that Christ has never separated himself from the Church. That witness is made concrete in the historical reality that, just as Christ never abandons his Church, so the priesthood, despite all attempts to eradicate it, has never abandoned the Church in this country. The priests who served and serve in Christ's name and in his place, continue to bear witness to his death and resurrection, to his sacrifice and his priesthood. They carry the inheritance of the seamless garment of Christ the priest.

That closeness to the Passion of Jesus is what the secular priest is called into at ordination, with all the blood, sweat, tears, spittle and mud that is the cost of sacrifice. In the sacrifice offered on the altar, that unique intimacy is renewed in the most precious way. The secular priest has a direct and unmediated connection to the Body and Blood of Christ. He wears the seamless garment of priesthood but it is a garment that does not remain spotless. It collects the dust of the road, the sweat of labour, the tears of grief, and often the spittle of mockery.

The priesthood is, in itself, a seamless garment. All priests are familiar with the analogy of four strands enmeshed in formation, but priesthood consists of more than four strands. It is more like a complex tapestry, a work of art that cannot hold together without all its many threads and intricate stitches. We continue to try to understand more deeply God's design in the fabric of priesthood, and to interpret the signs of its meaning. The seamless garment of priesthood is interwoven with threads of intimacy with Christ, of human wisdom, personal maturity and integrity, of trustful dialogue within and beyond the Church, and of continual exploration of the depths and heights of God. Without renewal of these threads it can become worn, torn, damaged and threadbare.

There is also in the secular priesthood, a seamlessness of continuity of tradition and connection with the local Church, with the diocese and with brother priests, that reaches across time, back into history and forwards to the generations that will come after. The seamless garment represents the tightly woven texture of generations of priesthood, and is the precious and unbreakable means of maintaining the continuity of the presence of Christ among his people throughout history. That seamless garment of continuous presence was torn, and its survival threatened in the sixteenth century. The seamless garment, it might be said, hung by a thread.

In a unique way, the secular priesthood of England and Wales ensured that the garment was not torn apart, some of them replicating Christ's own suffering and death in order to do so. The seamless garment of intimacy with Christ, of integrity and integration and of historical affinity has somehow been rewoven, mended, and reshaped over the generations since. What constitutes the priesthood in our own time is not a new garment, but a re-created one, patched and woven out of ancient threads. Those threads of sacrifice, of service, and of devotion to the people won by Christ's sacrifice are what bind, in a particular way, the priesthood to the community of Christ's faithful people in our lands.

> But you, you will be named 'priests of the Lord'. They will call you 'ministers of our God'. I will reward them faithfully and make an everlasting covenant with them. Their race will be famous throughout the nations, their descendants throughout the peoples. All who see them will admit that they are a race whom the Lord has blessed.
>
> *Isaiah 61: 6. 8-9 (from the first reading at the Chrism Mass)*

Endnotes

1   This is discussed in James Fearon, *What is Identity (as we now use the word)?*, 1999 (online pdf)

2   Apostolic Exhortation on the Priesthood, *Pastores Dabo Vobis*, Holy See, 1992, 31

3   Thanks to Mgr Peter Fleetwood for unravelling a densely worded passage in the original Latin

4   St Gregory the Great, 'Pastoral Care', trans. Henry Davis, *Ancient Christian writers: the Works of the Fathers in Translation*, Newman Press, Maryland and Longmans, Green & Co., London, 1978, pp 45-86

5   Hugh M Thomas, *The Secular Clergy in England 1066-1216*, Oxford University Press, Oxford, 2014, p 342

6   Tim Cooper, *The Last Generation of English Catholic Clergy: Parish Priests in the Diocese of Lichfield and Coventry in the Early Sixteenth Century*, Boydell Press, Bury St Edmunds, 1999, p 14

7   Vincent Nichols, *St John Fisher: Bishop and Theologian in Reformation and Controversy*, Alive Publications, Stoke on Trent, 2011, p 49

8   Christopher Haigh, *English Reformations: Religion, Politics and Society under the Tudors*, Clarendon Press, Oxford, 1993

9   Eamon Duffy, *The Stripping of the Altars: Traditional Religion in England 1400-1580*, Yale University Press, New Haven and London, 1992, pp 131-41

10   Peter Marshall, *The Catholic Priesthood and the English Reformation*, Clarendon Press, Oxford, 1994, p 100

11   Margaret Bowker, *The Secular Clergy in the Diocese of Lincoln 1495-1520*, Cambridge University Press, Cambridge, 1968, p 180

12   Robert Whiting, *Local Responses to the English Reformation*, Palgrave Macmillan, London, 1998, pp 24-6

13   Cooper, *Last Generation*, pp 30-6

14   Whiting, *Local Responses*, p 23

15   Thomas More, 'Apology', ed. J B Trapp, *Complete Works of St Thomas More* vol. 9, Yale University Press, 1979

16   Marshall, *Catholic Priesthood*, p 33

17   Whiting, *Local Responses*, pp 60-1

18   Helen Parish, 'It was never good world since ministers must have wyves': Clerical Celibacy, Clerical Marriage, and Anticlericalism in Reformation England', *Journal of Religious History* vol. 36 no1, March 2012, p 53

19   Marshall, *Catholic Priesthood*, pp 51-6

20   Parish, *Clerical Celibacy*, p 56

21 Helen Parish, *Clerical Marriage and the English Reformation: precedent, policy and practice*, Ashgate Press, Farnham, 2000, p 186

22 Whiting, *Local Responses*, pp 63-4

23 Eamon Duffy, *Fires of Faith: Catholic England under Mary Tudor*, Yale University Press, New Haven and London, 2009, p 23

24 Act of Uniformity, 1559, 1Eliz.Cap.2

25 Eamon Duffy, *Voices of Morebath: Reformation and Rebellion in an English Village*, Yale University Press, New Haven and London, 2001, p 175

26 Duffy, *Voices of Morebath,*, p 176

27 Parish, *Clerical Marriage*, p 200

28 Whiting, *Local Responses*, pp 68-70

29 David Rogers, 'English Recusants: some Medieval Literary Links', *Recusant History*, Vol 23, 1997, pp 483-507

30 Patrick McGrath & Joy Rowe, 'The Marian Priests under Elizabeth I', *Recusant History* vol. 17, 1984, pp 108-9

31 Eamon Duffy, 'Allen, William (1532–1594)', *Oxford Dictionary of National Biography*, Oxford University Press, 2004; online edn, Oct 2008 (http://www.oxforddnb.com/view/article/391, accessed 9 April 2016)

32 Eamon Duffy, 'Allen, William (1532–1594)', *Oxford Dictionary of National Biography*, op.cit.

33 For the text of the oath, see Michael E Williams, *The Venerable English College, Rome: a History*, Gracewing, Leominster, 2nd edition, 2008, p 289

34 Richard Challoner, *Memoirs of Missionary Priests, and of other Catholics of both sexes, that have suffered death in England on religious accounts, from the year 1577 to 1684*, (2 vols), 1742, many reprints

35 Alexandra Walsham, *Church Papists: Catholicism, Conformity and Confessional Polemic in Early Modern England*, Boydell Press, Bury St Edmunds, 1993, p 63

36 An Act Against Jesuits and Seminary Priests, 27 Elizabeth Cap 2

37 Paul Keane, *The Martyr's Crown: Rome and the English Church*, Family Publications, Oxford, 2009

38 Sarah Covington, 'Consolation on Golgotha: Comforters and Sustainers of dying priests in England 1580-1625', *Journal of Ecclesiastical History*, vol. 60 no 2, 2009, p 272

39 Covington p 283

40 Anne Dillon, *The Construction of Martyrdom in the English Catholic Community 1535-1603*, Ashgate Press, Farnham, 2002, p 107

41 Christopher Haigh, 'The Continuity of Catholicism in the English Reformation' in *The English Reformation Revised* ed. Haigh, Cambridge University Press, Cambridge, 1987

42 Michael Hodgetts, *Life at Harvington 1250-2000*, Archdiocese of Birmingham Historical Commission, 2002, p 23

43 Michael A Mullett, '"This Irreligious Art of Liing": Strategies of Disguise in Post-Reformation English Catholicism', *Journal of Historical Sociology*, vol. 20, no 3 September 2007, p 329

44 Mullett, *Strategies of Disguise*, p 336

45 Walsham, *Church Papists*, p 68

46 Peter Holmes, *Resistance and Compromise: the Political Thought of Elizabethan Catholics*, Cambridge University Press, Cambridge, 1982 (2009 reprint), p 108

47 William Allen, Letter to Catholics in England, 12 December 1592, in G Crosignanini, M Questier, T McCoog, *Recusancy and Conformity in Early Modern England: manuscript and printed sources in translation*, Pontifical Institute of Medieval Studies, Toronto, 2010, pp 260-2

48 See John Bossy, *Christianity in the West 1400-1700*, Oxford University Press (Opus), Oxford, 1985

49 Lisa McClain, 'Troubled Consciences: new understandings and performances of penance among Catholics in Protestant England', *Church History* No 82:1 March 2013, p 108

50 J D Crichton, *Worship in a Hidden Church*, Columba Press, Dublin, 1988, p 81

51 Michael Hodgetts, 'Recusant Liturgy 1559-1791', *Midland Catholic History*, 2011, pp 1-15

52 See Eamon Duffy, *Marking the Hours: English People and their Prayers 1240-1570*, Yale University Press, New Haven and London, 2006

53 Peter Holmes, 'Bishop, William (c.1554–1624)', *Oxford Dictionary of National Biography*, Oxford University Press, 2004 (http://www.oxforddnb.com/view/article/2474, accessed 9 April 2016)

54 Eamon Duffy, 'The English Secular Clergy and the Counter Reformation', *Journal of Ecclesiastical History*, vol. 34 No. 2 1983, pp 217-8

55 Duffy, *English Secular Clergy*, p 219

56 Michael Questier, 'Catholicism, Kinship and the Public Memory of Sir Thomas More', *Journal of Ecclesiastical History*, vol. 53 No. 3, July 2002, pp 476-509

57 William Sheils, 'Polemic as Piety: Thomas Stapleton's *Tres Thomae* and Catholic Controversy in the 1580s', *Journal of Ecclesiastical History*, vol. 60, No.1 2009, p 94

58 Peter Holmes, 'Bishop, William (c.1554–1624)', *Oxford Dictionary of National Biography*

59 Joseph Bergin, 'Smith, Richard (1567–1655)', *Oxford Dictionary of National Biography*, Oxford University Press, 2004 (http://www.oxforddnb.com/view/article/25886, accessed 9 April 2016)

60 Duffy, *Secular Clergy*, p 223

61 Duffy, *Secular Clergy*, p 228

62 Duffy, *Secular Clergy*, p 226

63 Duffy, *Secular Clergy*, p 227

64 Simon Johnson, *The English College at Lisbon: from Reformation to Toleration (vol. I)*, Downside Abbey Press, Stratton on the Fosse, 2015, p 255

65 Judith Champ, 'Cardinal Philip Howard OP, Rome, and English Recusancy', *New Blackfriars* vol. 76, June 1995, pp 272-3

66 Johnson, *Lisbon*, p 243

67 Johnson, *Lisbon*, p 245

68 Charles Dodd, *The Church History of England from the Year 1500 to the year 1688, to which is prefixed a general history of ecclesiastical affairs under British, Saxon and Norman Periods*, 1737-42 vol. 3, pp 482-4

69 Johnson, *Lisbon*, p 239

70 J C H Aveling, *The Handle and the Axe: the Catholic Recusants from Reformation to Emancipation*, Blond and Briggs, London, 1976, pp 312-3

71 John C Traver, 'Defoe, Unigenitus and the "Catholic Crusoe"', *Studies in English Literature 1500-1900*, vol. 51 No 3, 2011, pp 545-563

72 Edwin Burton, *The Life and Times of Bishop Challoner (1691-1781)*, Longmans, Green and Co., London, 1909, vol. I, p 36

73 Gabriel Glickman, *The English Catholic Community, 1688-1745: Politics, Culture and Ideology*, Boydell Press, Bury St Edmunds, 2009, p 202

74 Glickman, *English Catholic Community*, p 203

75 Burton, *Challoner*, vol. II, pp 120-1

76 Aveling, *Handle and the Axe*, p 323

77 Eamon Duffy, 'Richard Challoner 1691-1781: a memoir' in ed. Eamon Duffy, *Challoner and his Church: a Catholic Bishop in Georgian England*, Darton, Longman & Todd, London 1981, p 15

78 Burton, *Challoner* vol. II, p 9

[79] Mary Heimann, *Catholic Devotion in Victorian England*, Clarendon Press, Oxford, 1995, p 25

[80] Duffy, *Challoner*, p 21

[81] Eamon Duffy, 'A Rubb-up for old soares: Jesuits, Jansenists and the English Secular Clergy 1705-15' *Journal of Ecclesiastical History* vol. 28 No 3, 1977, p 308

[82] Gabriel Glickman, 'Gothic History and Catholic Enlightenment in the Works of Charles Dodd' (1672-1743), *The Historical Journal* Vol 54 No 2, 2011, p 349

[83] Dodd, *History*, vol. I, p 141

[84] Glickman, *Dodd*, p 356

[85] Joseph Berington, *The State and Behaviour of English Catholics, from the Reformation to the year 1780; with a view of their present number, wealth, character, etc.* 2 vols., London, 1780, p 148

[86] G. Hankin, *Life of Mary Anne Schimmelpenninck*, 2 vols., unknown publisher, 1858, p 36

[87] Eamon Duffy, *Joseph Berington and the English Catholic Cisalpine Movement, 1772-1803*, University of Cambridge PhD, 1973, p 218

[88] Crichton, *Worship in a Hidden Church*, p 96

[89] *The Tablet*, 31 January 1852

[90] Ushaw College Archives, LL1361, Lingard to John Walker, 16 November 1843

[91] *The Tablet*, 26 July 1851

[92] John Bossy, *The English Catholic Community 1570-1850*, Darton, Longman & Todd, London, 1975, pp 295-322

[93] V A McClelland, 'Changing Concepts of the Pastoral Office: Wiseman, Manning and the Oblates of St Charles', *Recusant History* vol. 25 No 2, 2000, pp 233-4

[94] Judith Champ, *William Bernard Ullathorne 1806-1889: a Different Kind of Monk*, Gracewing, Leominster, 2006, p 392

[95] Peter Doyle, *Correspondence of Alexander Goss, Bishop of Liverpool 1856-72*, Catholic Record Society, 2014, Preface, p xl

[96] Doyle, *Goss*, Preface, p xxxix

[97] 'The Catholic School, 7 June 1849', quoted in John T Smith, 'The Priest and the Elementary School in the Second Half of the Nineteenth Century', *Recusant History*, vol. 25, 2001, p 531

[98] John Smith, p 534

[99] Champ, *Ullathorne*, p 491

[100] Henry Edward Manning, *The Eternal Priesthood*, Burns Oates, London, 1883

[101] Quoted in McClelland, *Wiseman, Manning and the Oblates of St Charles*, pp 222-3

[102] Manning, *Eternal Priesthood*, pp 21-2

[103] Michael Williams, 'Seminaries and Priestly Formation', in eds. V A McClelland & Michael Hodgetts, *From Without the Flaminian Gate*, Darton, Longman Todd, London, 1999, p 69

[104] Manning, *Eternal Priesthood*, p 22

[105] John Henry Newman, 'The Infidelity of the Future' in ed. C Stephen Dessain, *Catholic Sermons of Cardinal Newman*, Burns Oates, London, 1957, pp 117-34

[106] Williams, *Seminaries and Priestly Formation*, p 73

[107] Herbert Vaughan, *The Young Priest*, ed. John Vaughan, Burns Oates, London, 1904, pp 26-29

[108] Judith Champ, *Pope Benedict XVI, St Mary's College, Oscott and the Venerable Bartholomew Holzhauser*, Gracewing, Leominster, 2010, p 20

[109] Champ, *Holzhauser*, pp 49-71

[110] James Abbott, 'The Apostolic Union', *The Furrow*, vol. 6 No 7, July 1955

111 Mark Vickers, *By the Thames Divided: Cardinal Bourne in Southwark and Westminster*, Gracewing, Leominster, 2013, p 42

112 Williams, *Seminaries and Priestly Formation*, p 72

113 Vickers, p 70

114 John Sharp, 'Oscott in Oxford – Lost Opportunity of Misguided Pipe Dream?' *Recusant History* vol. 30, 2010, p 329

115 Sharp, *Oscott in Oxford*, p 330

116 Obituary quoted in Judith Champ, *A Seminary Goes to War: St Mary's College, Oscott and the First World War*, Oscott Publications, 2015, p 87

117 Michael Hornsby Smith, *Roman Catholics in England: Studies in Social Structure since the Second World War*, Cambridge University Press, Cambridge, 1987, p 32

118 Denis Gwynn, 'Growth of the Catholic Community', in ed. George Andrew Beck, *The English Catholics 1850-1950*, Burns Oates, London, 1950, p 436

119 John Dunford, *Practical Suggestions for the Newly Ordained* (preface by Cardinal Bourne), Burns, Oates and Washbourne, London, 1930

120 Dunford, p 16

121 Dunford, pp 118-121

122 Ronald Knox, *The Priestly Life*, Sheed and Ward, London, 1959, pp 69-80

123 Knox, p 77

124 Dunford, p 81

125 John Carmel Heenan, *Council and Clergy*, Chapman, London, 1966, p 108

126 Heenan, p 77

127 James D Crichton, *Servants of the People: today's priest in the light of the Second Vatican Council*, St Paul, London, 1990, pp 12-13

128 George Beck, 'Today and Tomorrow', in ed. Beck, p 610

129 Donald MacRaild, *The Irish Diaspora in Britain, 1750-1939*, Palgrave Macmillan, London, 2010, pp 77-8

130 MacRaild, p 61

131 Steven Fielding, *Class and Ethnicity: Irish Catholics in England 1880-1939*, Open University Press, London, 1992, p 43

132 Margaret Turnham, *Catholic Faith and Practice in England 1779-1992: the role of Revivalism and Renewal*, Boydell Press, Bury St Edmunds, 2015

133 Miki Garcia, *Rebuilding London: Irish Migrants in Post-War Britain*, The History Press, Dublin, 2015, p 9

134 Garcia, p 19

135 Garcia, p 114

136 Garcia, p 24

137 Brian Van Hove, 'Jansenism and Ireland', *Homiletics and Pastoral Review*, 24 February 2015

138 Fielding, p 44

139 Fielding, p 46

140 Hornsby Smith, *Roman Catholics in England*, pp 24-5

141 Desmond Ryan, *The Catholic Parish: Institutional Discipline, Tribal Identity and Religious Development in the English Church*, Sheed and Ward, London, 1996, p 137

142 Mary Jane Smith, *The Priest's Life – a Survey of Training and other Factors contributing to the well-being of Catholic Priests*, University of Birmingham M.Phil., 1996, p 59

143 Quoted in ed. Michael Hornsby Smith, *Catholics in England 1950-2000: historical and sociological perspectives*, Continuum, London and New York, 1999, p 52

144 Antony Archer, *The Two Catholic Church: a Study in Oppression*, SCM Press, London, 1986, pp 163-9

145 Robert Towler, 'The Role of the Clergy', in N Lash and J Rhymer, *The Christian Priesthood*, Darton Longman Todd, London, 1970

146 Towler, p 178

147 Hornsby Smith, *Roman Catholic Beliefs in England: Customary Catholicism and Transformations of Authority*, Cambridge University Press, Cambridge, 1991, p 147

148 Hornsby Smith, *Roman Catholic Beliefs*, p 190

149 George Scott, *The RCs: a Report on Roman Catholics in Britain Today*, Hutchinson, London, 1967, p 181

150 Archivum Venerabilis Collegii Anglorum de Urbe (AVCAU), Scr. 87/6, G Tindall, *A Report drawn up for the 1958 conference on priestly vocations in Vienna*, 13 November 1958

151 AVCAU, Scr. 87/6

152 AVCAU Scr. 107/11, *Circular Letter to Bishops on the occasion of the first centenary of the death of the Curé d'Ars concerning certain problems of ecclesiastical formation*, 5 June 1959

153 AVCAU Scr. 87/11, *Letter to Bishops concerning the problem of Ecclesiastical Vocation and the Diocesan work for fostering Priestly Vocations*, 11 February 1960

154 AVCAU Scr. 107/2 part II, *Motu Proprio, establishing the Pontifical Society for Priestly Vocations in the Sacred Congregation for Seminaries and Universities of Studies* (typescript English translation), 1941

155 AVCAU Scr. 107/4, *Papers prepared for first international congress of Vocations Directors*, December 1966

156 Scott, *The RCs*, p 175

157 Scott, *The RCs*, p 178

158 Michael Hodgetts, 'The Iron Form: Catholics and Philosophy between the Councils', in *From Without the Flaminian Gate*, pp 84-107

159 Scott, *The RCs*, p 180

160 John Carmel Heenan, *Council and Clergy*, Chapman, London, 1966

161 Heenan, *Council and Clergy*, p 105

162 Heenan, *Council and Clergy*, p 78

163 Heenan, *Council and Clergy*, p 98

164 AVCAU Scr. 107/5, *The Future of Junior Seminaries in the North of England: a report of discussions at Ushaw*, 1970

165 Scott, *The RCs*, p 207

166 For a discussion of English lay Catholic experience of faith and practice in this period, see Alana Harris, *Faith in the Family: a lived religious history of English Catholicism 1945-82*, Manchester University Press, Manchester and New York, 2013, p 108

167 Michael Hollings, *Living Priesthood*, Mayhew McCrimmon, Essex, 1977

168 Hollings, p 237

169 Hollings, p 239

170 Hollings, p 239

171 Robin Gill, *The Myth of the Empty Church*, SPCK, London, 1996, pp 293-4

172 Hornsby Smith, *Roman Catholics in England*, pp 189-90

173 *The Tablet*, 13 October 1990

174 Harris, *Faith in the Family*, pp 233-50

175 Hornsby Smith, *Catholics in England 1950-2000*, p 13

176 *The Sign We Give: Report from a Working Party on Collaborative Ministry*, Bishops' Conference of England and Wales, Matthew James Publishing, Essex, 1995

177 Quoted in Hornsby Smith, *Catholics in England 1950-2000*, p 16

178 *The Sign We Give*, p 10

179 *The Sign We Give*, p 23

180 Harris, *Faith in the Family*, p 113

181 Mullett, *Strategies of Disguise*, p 336

182 S H Louden and L J Francis, *The Naked Parish Priest: what priests really think they're doing*, Continuum, London, 2003. The Bishops' Conference of England and Wales and the National Conference of Priests rejected the book's broad findings as 'not a true

reflection of the current beliefs of priests in England and Wales'; C Fallon, *Who do we think we are? A Study of the Self-understandings of priests in the Roman Catholic Archdiocese of Liverpool*, PhD, University of Durham, 2013, p 96, n 243

183 Louden and Francis, *The Naked Parish Priest*, pp 95-8, 206

184 Fallon, *Who do we think we are?* p 118

185 Mullett, *Strategies of Disguise*, p 329

186 Michael Richards, *A People of Priests*, Darton Longman Todd, London, 1995, p 15

187 Richards, *A People of Priests*, pp 113-4

188 Richards, *A People of Priests*, p 114

189 Donal O'Leary, *New Hearts for New Models: a spirituality for priests today*, Columba Press, Dublin, 1997, p 13

190 O'Leary, *New Hearts*, pp 19-20

191 O'Leary, *New Hearts*, pp 110-11

192 Tony Philpot, *Priesthood in Reality*, Kevin Mayhew, Bury St Edmunds, 1998, p 6

193 Philpot, *Priesthood in Reality*, pp 7-11

194 Heenan, *Council and Clergy*, p 98

195 Philpot, *Priesthood in Reality*, p 74

196 Philpot, *Priesthood in Reality*, p 77

197 Hornsby Smith, *Catholics in England, 1950-2000*, p 304

198 Desmond Ryan, *The Catholic Parish: Institutional Discipline, Tribal Identity and Religious Development in the English Church*, Sheed and Ward, London, 1996

199 Ryan, *The Catholic Parish*, p 2

200 Ryan, *The Catholic Parish*, p 199

201 Ryan, *The Catholic Parish*, p 304

202 Mary Jane Smith, *The Priest's Life – a Survey of Training and other Factors contributing to the well-being of Catholic Priests*, University of Birmingham M.Phil., 1996

203 Ryan, *The Catholic Parish*, p 150

204 Ryan, *The Catholic Parish*, p 179

205 Harris, p 260

206 Hornsby Smith, *Catholics in England, 1950-2000*, p 304

207 *Pastores Dabo Vobis*, 31

208 Hornsby Smith, *Roman Catholics in England, 1950-2000*, p 205

209 Philip Sheldrake, *Explorations in Spirituality: History, Theology and Social Practice*, Paulist Press, New York, 2010, p 24

210 Sheldrake, *Explorations*, p 25

211 *The Tablet*, 23 May 1970

212 Harris, *Faith in the Family*, p 248

213 Ryan, *The Catholic Parish*, p 199

214 *Homily of Pope Francis at Mass at Santa Marta*, 30 April 2015, accessed at www.vatican.va

215 Chris Lowney, *Pope Francis: Why He Leads the Way He Does*, Loyola Press, Chicago, 2013, p 105

216 John O'Donohue quoted in Donal O'Leary, *New Hearts for New Models*, pp 97-102

217 O'Leary, *New Hearts*, p 103

218 Philpot, *Priesthood in Reality*, p 46

219 Sherry Turkle, *Reclaiming Conversation: the Power of Talk in a Digital Age*, Penguin Press, New York, 2015, pp 21-2

220 Turkle, *Reclaiming Conversation*, p 23

221 Turkle, *Reclaiming Conversation*, p 61

222 John Armstrong, *In Search of Civilisation: Remaking a Tarnished Idea*, Penguin, London, 2010, pp 146-7

223 Tony Philpot, *Brothers in Christ: a call to Fraternity in the Diocesan Priesthood*, Kevin Mayhew, Suffolk, 1991, p 12

224 Theodore Zeldin, *Conversation*, The Harvill Press, London, 1998, p 14

225 Philpot, *Brothers in Christ*, p 13

226 *Presbyterium Ordinis*, Section II, 49

227 *The Code of Canon Law*, 1983, Can. 278.2

228 Can 280

229 Can. 245.2

230 *Pastores Dabo Vobis,* 230

231 *Directory on the Life and Ministry of Priests,* The Holy See, 1994, 26

232 *Directory on the Life and Ministry of Priests, 24*

233 *Directory on the Life and Ministry of Priests, 25*

234 *Directory on the Life and Ministry of Priests, 25*

235 Anthony J Gittins, 'Discipleship is not Self-Taught' in *Religious Life Review,* vol. 54, Jan/Feb 2015, pp 37-8

236 Robert K Greenleaf, *Servant Leadership,* 1970, accessed on www.mindtools.com

237 See p 26

238 Michael White and Tom Corcoran, *Rebuilt: Awakening the Faithful, Reaching the Lost and Making Church Matter,* Ave Maria Press, Indiana, 2013

239 *Address of Pope Francis at the ceremony commemorating the fiftieth anniversary of the institution of the Synod of Bishops,* 17 October 2015, accessed at www.vatican.va

240 *Address of Pope Francis at the Fifth National Ecclesial Congress of the Church in Italy,* 5 November 2015, accessed at www.zenit.org

241 Lowney, *Pope Francis,* p 114

242 *Address of Pope Francis at the Fifth National Ecclesial Congress of the Church in Italy,* 5 November 2015, accessed at www.zenit.org

Index